MW00952819

1

Dear readers, I am happy to present my book, in which I want to share my five-year experience's worth of cooking with an Air fryer.

I like to eat deliciously, like in a restaurant, but I also love when a dish is cooked at home on its own, preferably quickly and without much effort. Also, I want the food that I eat to be healthy, though I'm not on a diet and sometimes eat fatty foods and sweet desserts.

Recipes were selected for this book based on these wishes. All recipes in this book were prepared and tasted before being printed on the pages of this book. Only delicious recipes were included in this book.

The next factor in selecting recipes for this book is the simplicity of their cooking.

Most of the recipes from this book served in restaurants around the world. However, most of these recipes are easy to prepare, and it only takes a little time. Just a few simple steps, such as peeling, cutting, pouring, mixing, sprinkle with oil, make breading and most dishes will be ready in 10 minutes.

Hot dishes are fresh from the oven with only a few drops of oil for frying.

*The photos.*

I did not overload the book with photos but for each recipe you will find a photo of the cooked dish. For most recipes, one photo is enough that there are no questions left on how to prepare it, just follow directions and a list of ingredients in the recipe. However sometimes it will be useful to see more, therefore in some recipes, you will find a few photos that will help you in preparing the dish, and you will be able to cook everything deliciously!

Note. This book is structured for convenient use and easy understanding how to cook a dish. The book divided into chapters by types of products. Including the recipes from pork, beef, poultry, seafood, vegetables, snacks, burger recipes and dessert dishes.

Also, you will find brief information right under the photo of the recipe, before the list of ingredients and directions.

*Prep Time* means how long it will take to prepare the necessary ingredients until the moment when you need to put your products in air fryer

*Cook Time* means the remaining time during which the dish will be cooked.

*Servings* means how many people or how many pieces will come from the ingredients specified in the recipe. When the recipe says 1 Serving, you can increase all the ingredients twice and cook for two. In this case, you need to increase the cooking time by approximately 20%.

*Temp* in some models of air fryers temperature is indicated in Celsius in others by Fahrenheit, also the step of temperature change can be different 5 or 10 degrees. For comfort cooking, I indicated the cooking temperature in Celsius and Fahrenheit with rounding to the higher side where necessary.

## Preparing Difficulty

In the main, the recipes in this book are simple to make. Just mix some spices, grind them meat/fish/vegetables then cook at a specific temperature and time. Such recipes are noted in the book like *No Skill Required*

For some recipes, you will need to remove the skin from the fish, make a bread pan for shrimp, cut the meat into steaks, etc. Such recipes noted in the book like *Requires Minimum Skill*

Recipes in which you need to work with dough or recipes where you need to stuff some foods noted in the book like *Requires Specific Skill*


## Overall notes for some recipes

**Butter** everywhere in the recipes it means Salted Butter, but you can use Unsalted Butter which will not much change the taste of the dish. However, the salted butter stored longer.

**Milk** - Long life milk in cartons. But if you use Fresh Milk this will only improve the taste, especially for baking.

**Salt** in my recipes, except for Asian recipes, I use salt less than average, because I love low salt cooking. You can put 50% more from the specified amount or you can salt the prepared dish after serving if you like more salty foods.

All recipes in this book are suitable for most models of air fryers.

Pay attention to the fullness of the basket of your air fryer. If the basket is too full, it is possible that the dish will be cooked longer than the required time and it may be necessary to mix the products on halfway additionally.

In the dessert recipes, the number of cookies shown in the recipe may vary depending on the size of the cookies.

In most recipes, I use room temperature ingredients

In those recipes where you need to beat the butter with sugar, essences, oils use hand mixer on medium-high speed. In those recipes where it is necessary to whip dry flour mixes in a separate bowl, use hand mixer on medium-low speed.

All the rest of the information for making tasty, useful and straightforward dishes you will find inside the book.

I hope this book will be convenient and useful for you, your family and friends. I'll be happy about this.

Bon Appetit!

# CHAPTER ONE PORK MEAT RECIPES

## BBQ Pork Ribs

*Prep Time 10 minutes // Cook Time 15 minutes*
*Servings 4//Temp 180ºC or 360ºF//Requires Minimum Skill*

**Ingredients**

1 ½ lb. of pork ribs

3 garlic cloves, chopped

4 tablespoon of BBQ sauce

1 tablespoon of honey

1/4 teaspoon of cinnamon

1/4 teaspoon of fennel

1 teaspoon of olive oil

1/2 teaspoon of salt

1 teaspoon of pepper

1 teaspoon of soy sauce

## Directions

Wash and chop pork ribs into small pieces.

### *In a mixing bowl*

Add garlic, BBQ sauce, honey, cinnamon, fennel, olive oil, salt, pepper and soy sauce and mix well.

Grind and pour the pork ribs into a spicy mixture and place bowl with marinated meats in fridge for at least 4 hours.

Preheat the air fryer for 5 minutes at 180°C or 360°F

Place into air fryer basket a parchment baking paper or baking mat, so less fat will drip down and the basket will remain cleaner. Grease pork ribs with a thin layer of marinade mixture and put the meats on baking paper using the tongs.

Fry for 15 minutes at 180°C or 360°F and then turn ribs, grease of rest marinade and fry for another 10 minutes at 180°C or 360°F

## Buttered Garlic Pork Chops

*Prep Time 10 minutes // Cook Time 15 minutes*

*Servings 2//Temp 175ºC or 350ºF//Requires Minimum Skill*

## Ingredients

4 pork chops

1 tablespoon of coconut butter refined

1 tablespoon of coconut oil

3 garlic cloves, grated

2 teaspoons of parsley

½ teaspoon of salt

½ teaspoon of pepper

## Directions

Flavor the pork chops with 1/2 tsp. of salt on both sides and keep aside.

### In a mixing bowl

Add the coconut oil and butter, grated garlic, parsley, salt and pepper. Mix well with a fork.

Grease the pork chops into a spicy mixture and wrap up in aluminum foil for food, then fridge for an hour.

After one hour remove chops from the food foil and if there is any spare mixture in the foil then grease it over the chops.

Preheat the air fryer for 5 minutes at 175ºC or 350ºF

Put pork chops on the grill mat into the air fryer basket and fry for 7 minutes on one side and then 8 minutes on another at 175ºC or 350ºF.

Serve with fried vegetables and favorite sauce. Spray with some extra olive oil.

# Crispy Pork Chops

*Prep Time 10 minutes // Cook Time 12 minutes*

*Servings 3//Temp 205°C or 400°F//Requires Minimum Skill*

## Ingredients

3 centers cut boneless pork chops, fat trimmed, about 3/4-inch thick and 5 oz. each.

1 large egg, beaten

1/2 cup of panko crumbs

1/3 cup of cornflakes crumbs, crushed

1 oz. of parmesan cheese, grated

1 teaspoon of sweet paprika

1/2 teaspoon of garlic powder

1/2 teaspoon of onion powder

1/4 teaspoon of chilli powder

1/2 teaspoon of salt

1/8 teaspoon of black pepper

1 tablespoon of olive oil for spray

## Directions

Flavor the pork chops with ½ tsp. of salt on both sides and keep aside.

### *In a mixing bowl*

Add panko and cornflake crumbs, parmesan cheese, paprika, garlic powder, onion powder, chilli powder, black pepper, pinch of salt and mix well with a fork or spoon.

*In a plate* place the beaten egg.

Dip the pork chops into the egg, then into panko mixture.

Preheat the air fryer for 10 minutes at 205°C or 400°F

Spray the oil in air fryer basket and both sides on chops.

Fry for 14 minutes at 205°C or 400°F

Serve with fried vegetables and favorite sauce.

## Cantonese Fried Pork.

*Prep Time 10 minutes + refrigerate for 2 hrs. for marinade*

*Cook Time 15 minutes // Servings 4*

*Temp 170 - 205ºC or 340 – 400ºF // No Skill Requires*

## Ingredients

2 lbs. of pork means

1/3 cup soy sauce

2 tbsp. of sugar

1 tbsp. of honey

½ tbsp. of salt

## Directions

Cut 2 lbs of pork meats into 1.5" width

Add 1/3 cup of soy sauce

Add 2 tbsp of sugar

Add 1 tbsp of honey

Add ½ tbsp. of salt

Massage the meat marinade for 2 minutes

Cover and refrigerate meats for 2 hours or overnight

Add meats into the air fryer

Fry meats for 10 minutes at 170°C or 340°F

Caramelize meats for 5 minutes at 205°C or 400°F in air fryer

Cut into slices and serve.

*Tip: cook for a few minutes if meats are not cooked.*

# Chinese Pork Chops and Jalapeño Peppers

*Prep Time 10min+20min for marinate // Cook Time 18 min*

*Servings 4//Temp180-205ºC or 360-400ºF//Requires Minimum Skill*

## Ingredients

2 lb. of pork chops

1 egg white

1 teaspoon of sea salt

1/2 teaspoon black pepper freshly ground

3/4 cup of cornstarch

2 Jalapeño pepper stems removed, sliced

2 green onions, sliced

2 tablespoons of Peanut oil

## Directions

Slice pork chops into cutlet pieces, leaving a little on the bones and pat dry.

### *In a mixing bowl*

Add egg white, 1/2 tsp. of salt and 1/4 tsp. of pepper and whisk until foamy.

Dip pork chop pieces to egg white mixture and coat thoroughly. Keep aside for at least 20 minutes.

### *In another mixing bowl*

Add cornstarch and shift pork chops. Mix well the pork chops in the cornstarch. Shake off pork and spray with bit of oil.

Spray little of oil into the basket and preheat air fryer for 5 minutes at 180°C or 360°F.

Fry for 15 minutes at 180°C or 360°F.

While meat is being cooked,

Chop green onions and slice Jalapeños peppers thin and remove seeds. Salt and pepper the chopped greens.

After 15 minutes remove the basket and stir meat well with tongs. Add chopped greens, mix well again and fry for 3 – 5 minutes at 205°C or 400°F.

## Honey Mustard Pork Meatballs

*Prep Time 10 minutes // Cook Time 14 minutes*

*Servings 4//Temp 200ºC or 390ºF//Requires Specific Skill*

## Ingredients

12 oz. of minced pork meat

2 oz. of onion, peeled and diced

1 teaspoon of mustard

1 teaspoon of honey

1 teaspoon of garlic, fine chopped

1 tablespoon of cheddar cheese, grated

1 tablespoon of fresh basil, fine chopped

Pinch of salt

Pinch of pepper

## Directions

### *In a mixing bowl*

Add meat, onion, mustard, honey (optional), chopped garlic and basil, grated cheese and mix it well.

Roll forcemeat into small balls and keep aside.

Spray little oil into air fryer basket and onto meatballs.

Preheat the air fryer for 3 minutes at 200°C or 390°F

Fry for 14 minutes at 200°C or 390°F

Serve with fried vegetables and favorite sauce.

*Tip - Wet your hands with water, so that the mince does not stick to your hands.*

# Maple Syrup Pork Chops

*Prep Time 10 minutes // Cook Time 20 minutes*

*Servings 4//Temp 205°C or 400°F//Requires Minimum Skill*

## Ingredients

4 pork chops. You can take on the bone, and without it, for example, cut the pork neck into pieces about an inch thick.

7 fl.oz. of Maple syrup.

2 fl.oz. of grape or apple cider vinegar.

3 garlic cloves, crushed

¼ teaspoon of salt

1 teaspoon of pepper freshly ground.

## Directions

### In a mixing bowl

Add maple syrup, vinegar, crushed garlic, salt and ground pepper and mix well with a fork.

Grease the meat pieces in maple mixture using a silicone brush for cooking. Keep aside minimum at 30 minutes or longer. Save the remaining marinade for frying.

Preheat the air fryer for 5 minutes at 205°C or 400°F

Place into air fryer basket a parchment baking paper. Grease pork chops with a thin layer of maple marinade and put the meats on baking paper using the tongs.

Fry for 10 minutes at 205°C or 400°F, and then pull out the basket and grease chops with brush. Reduce the temperature at 180°C or 360°F and fry another 5 minutes.

After 15 minutes total turn meats, grease and fry until golden brown, about 5 minutes.


As a side dish, fresh or fried vegetables, French fries or baked potatoes are very good.

## Mustard Garlic Pork Tenderloin

*Prep Time 10 minutes // Cook Time 15 minutes*

*Servings 4//Temp 205ºC or 400ºF//Requires Minimum Skill*

## Ingredients

1 lb. of pork tenderloin, sliced about 5x5 inch pieces into 1 inch thick

1 cup of breadcrumbs

1 ½ teaspoons of salt

1 teaspoon of black pepper

2 tablespoon of honey

2 tablespoon of mustard

2 fl.oz. of water

1 teaspoon of ground ginger

3 garlic cloves, crushed

Pinch of cayenne pepper

## Directions

Flavor the pork chops with salt and pepper on both sides and keep aside.

## *In a mixing bowl*

Add mustard, water, ginger, garlic, honey and cayenne pepper and mix well with fork.

Dip each pork pieces into the spice-mixture, then press each side into the breadcrumbs coating evenly.

Preheat the air fryer for 5 minutes at 205°C or 400°F

Spray the oil in air fryer basket and both sides on panko meat.

Fry for 10 minutes at 205°C or 400°F, and then turn meats and fry until golden brown, about 5 minutes.

Serve with potatoes or vegetables and favorite sauce.

# Pork Tenderloin with Bell Pepper and Onions

*Prep Time 10 minutes // Cook Time 20 minutes*

*Servings 4 // Temp 205ºC or 400ºF //No Skill Requires*

## Ingredients

1 1/2 lb. of pork tenderloin

2 bell pepper cut into cubes about 2 inches

2 red onions cut into cubes about 2 inches

1/2 teaspoon of rosemary

1/2 teaspoon of thyme

1/2 teaspoon of marjoram

1/2 teaspoon of basil

¼ teaspoon of salt

1 teaspoon of pepper freshly ground

1 tablespoon of olive oil

½ tablespoon mustard

## Directions

### *In the oven dish*

Add the bell pepper and the onion squares, rosemary, thyme, basil, marjoram, salt and pepper, pour in ½ tablespoon of olive oil and mix well.

Cut the pork tenderloin into pieces about 3 inches and grate with salt, pepper, and mustard. Spray onto the pieces with olive oil and put meats into the oven dish on top of the pepper and onion cubes mix.

Preheat the air fryer for 5 minutes at 205°C or 400°F

Place into air fryer basket an oven dish with meats and spiced greens.

Fry for 10 minutes at 205°C or 400°F, and then pull out the basket and stir all ingredients well.

Reduce the temperature at 180°C or 360°F and fry for another 10 minutes.

Serve with mashed potatoes and a fresh salad.

## Spicy Thai Meatballs

*Prep Time 5 minutes // Cook Time 15 minutes*
*Servings 4//Temp 180ºC or 360ºF//Requires Minimum Skill*

## Ingredients

14 oz. of pork mince

1 large onion puree

1 teaspoon of garlic puree or rubbed garlic

1 tablespoon of soy sauce

1 tablespoon of Worcester sauce

2 teaspoons of Thai Kitchen Red Curry Paste

½ Lime rind and juice

½ teaspoon of cinnamon

1 teaspoon of Chinese seasoning

1 teaspoon of coriander

Pinch of salt & pepper

## Directions

### *In a mixing bowl*

Add all ingredients mix well with spatula or hands.

Roll forcemeat into small balls and keep aside.

Spray little oil into air fryer basket and onto meatballs.

Preheat the air fryer for 3 minutes at 200°C or 390°F

Fry for 15 minutes at 180°C or 360°F

Serve with fry vegetables and favorite sauce.

# CHAPTER TWO BEEF MEAT RECIPES

## Beef Meatloaf Flavored With Black Pepper

*Prep Time 10 minutes // Cook Time 25 minutes*
*Servings 4 // Temp 180ºC or 360ºF // Requires Minimum Skill*

### Ingredients

2 lb. of minced beef

1 large onion peeled and diced

3 tablespoons of tomato ketchup

1 teaspoon of Worcester sauce

1 tablespoon of dried oregano

1 tablespoon of dried basil

1 tablespoon of dried parsley

¼ teaspoon of salt

½ teaspoon of pepper

7 oz. of breadcrumbs

## Directions

### *In a mixing bowl*

Add the mince, onion, herbs, tomato ketchup and Worcester sauce and mix well with hands or using spatula about five minutes massaging and mixing the ingredients

*It is important because no one wants to get with one slice of meatloaf that has too much spice on, or to get one slice with no seasoning.*

Then add the breadcrumbs and mix well again.

From the forcemeat make the form of a pie or put in a suitable baking dish.

Preheat the air fryer for 3 minutes at 180°C or 360°F

Fry for 25 minutes at 180°C or 360°F

Serve with favorite sauce and fry potatoes and vegetables.

*Tip: add a piece of parchment paper into the air fryer tray and you will be easier to wash the basket.*

# Crumbed Schnitzel

*Prep Time 5 minutes // Cook Time 12 minutes*

*Servings 2//Temp 180ºC or 360ºF//Requires Minimum Skill*

## Ingredients

2 thin beef schnitzel about 5 oz. each one

2 tablespoons of olive oil

4 oz. of breadcrumbs

1 egg, whisked

¼ teaspoon of black pepper powder

¼ teaspoon of salt

2 lemon slices to serve

## Directions

### In a mixing bowl

Add breadcrumbs, olive oil, salt and pepper and mix well until the mixture becomes loose and crumbly.

### In a plate place the beaten egg.

Dip the schnitzels into the egg, then into the crumb mixture making sure it is evenly and fully covered.

Preheat air fryer for 5 minutes at 180°C or 360°F

Put the schnitzels in air fryer basket and fry for 12 minutes at 180°C or 360°F

Serve immediately with lemon slices on top.

## Juicy Veal Steak

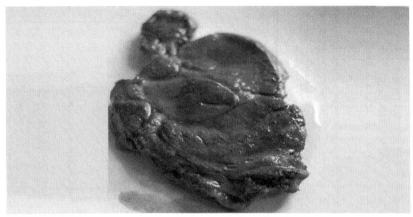

*Prep Time 5 minutes // Cook Time 6 minutes*
*Servings 4//Temp 180ºC or 360ºF//Requires Minimum Skill*

## Ingredients

4 thin tenderloin veal steaks about 4 oz. each one

1 tablespoon of olive oil

½ teaspoon of black pepper freshly ground

½ teaspoon of oregano

½ teaspoon of salt

## Directions

### *Take the steak on the table or a large plate*

Grate steaks with olive oil, oregano, salt and freshly ground black pepper. Distribute evenly all these spices on the both sides of the steak.

*For medium rate steak.*

Preheat air fryer for 5 minutes at 180°C or 360°F

Place the parchment for baking or baking mat in air fryer basket and put the steak on top.

Fry for 3 minutes at 180°C or 360°F and then turn stakes and fry for another 3 minutes at 180°C or 360°F.

After 6 minutes at all take the steak out of the air fryer and place it on a plate.

Let steaks cool down for another 3 minutes.

Done.

## Meatballs on Sticks

*Prep Time 10 minutes // Cook Time 15 minutes*

*Servings 24 // Temp 190ºC or 375ºF // Requires Min Skill*

## Ingredients

1 lb. of mince beef

6 fl.oz. of tomato ketchup

1 tablespoon of <u>Tabasco sauce</u>

2 ½ tablespoons of <u>Worcester sauce</u>

¼ cup of vinegar

1 tablespoon of lemon juice

½ cup of brown sugar

½ teaspoon of dry Mustard

4 oz. of breadcrumbs.

## Directions

Take set of <u>wooden sticks for food</u> about 4''– 5'' and soak them in water for 15 minutes

### *In a mixing bowl*

Add ketchup, sauces, vinegar, lemon juice, sugar, mustard and mix well.

Add the mince and breadcrumbs to the bowl and mix well with hands or using spatula so that all is evenly coated.

Form into medium-sized meatballs using spoon or only with hands and place them into air fryer basket.

Preheat the air fryer for 3 minutes at 190°C or 375°F

Fry for 15 minutes at 190°C or 375°F

Serve with favorite sauce.

# Rib Eye Steak

*Prep Time 5 minutes // Cook Time 10 minutes*

*Servings 2//Temp 180°C or 360°F//Requires Skill*

## Ingredients

2 Rib eye Steak about 8 oz. each one

1 tablespoon of olive oil

½ teaspoon of white pepper freshly ground

½ teaspoon of oregano

½ teaspoon of salt

2 sprig of thyme

## Directions

### Take the steak on the table or a large plate

Grate steaks with olive oil, oregano, salt and freshly ground white pepper. Distribute evenly all these spices on the both sides of the steak.

Preheat air fryer for 5 minutes at 180ºC or 360ºF

Put the steak into air fryer and put on top a sprig of thyme

Fry for 8 minutes at 180ºC or 360ºF and then turn stakes with thyme springs on top and fry for another 7 minutes at 180ºC or 360ºF.

*Tip The time for medium well roast indicated. You can fry more or less for 2 to 4 minutes, depending on your preference for the degree of roast meat.*

## Strip Steak with Fried Potatoes

*Prep Time 10 minutes // Cook Time 30 minutes*

*Servings 4//Temp 180-200ºC or 360-390ºF//Requires Minimum Skill*

## Ingredients

7 oz. Beef Striploin Steak

4 medium potatoes chopped

1 tablespoon of olive oil

½ teaspoon of white pepper freshly ground

¼ teaspoon of white pepper powder

½ teaspoon of basil

½ teaspoon of oregano

¼ teaspoon of thyme

¼ teaspoon of garlic powder

¼ teaspoon of dill dried weed powder

1 teaspoon of salt

## Directions

### *In a mixing bowl*

Add potatoes, ½ tbsp. olive oil, ¼ tsp white pepper powder, ½ tsp basil, ¼ tsp garlic powder, ¼ tsp dill dried weed powder, ½ tsp salt and mix well.

Preheat air fryer for 5 minutes at 180ºC or 360ºF

Put spiced potatoes in air fryer basket.

Cook for 18 minutes. After 10 minutes remove the basket and stir potatoes to uniformly brown.

Once done, remove the cooked potatoes from the basket and put aside.

### *Take the steak on the table or a large plate*

Grate ½ tbsp. oil, ½ tsp salt, ½ tsp freshly ground white pepper, ½ tsp oregano and ¼ tsp of thyme. Distribute evenly all these spices on the both sides of the steak.

Put the steak into air fryer and fry for 12 minutes 200ºC or 390ºF.

Serve with the roasted potatoes

*Tip The time for medium well roast indicated. You can fry more or less for 2 to 4 minutes, depending on your preference for the degree of roast meat.*

## Spicy Beef Meatballs

*Prep Time 5 minutes // Cook Time 15 minutes*

*Servings 4 // Temp 180ºC or 360ºF // Requires Minimum Skill*

## Ingredients

14 oz. of beef mince

1 large onion puree

1 teaspoon of garlic puree or rubbed garlic

½ teaspoon of cinnamon

1 teaspoon of coriander

1 tablespoon of breadcrumbs

Pinch of salt

Pinch of black pepper, powder

Pinch of chili pepper, powder

## Directions

### *In a mixing bowl*

Add all ingredients mix well with spatula or hands.

Roll forcemeat into small balls and keep aside.

Spray little oil into air fryer basket and onto meatballs.

Preheat the air fryer for 5 minutes at 180°C or 360°F

Fry for 15 minutes at 180°C or 360°F

Serve with fry potatoes and favorite sauce.

# Top Sirloin Garlic Steaks

*Prep Time 10 min+4 hour marinate // Cook Time 10 minutes*
*Servings 4//Temp 180-200ºC or 360-390ºF//Requires Minimum Skill*

## Ingredients

1 lb. of beef sirloin steaks

6 cloves of garlic peeled and chopped

1 teaspoon of olive oil

1/4 teaspoon of black pepper freshly ground

1/4 teaspoon of salt

1 tbsp. of coriander leaves, chopped (optional)

## Directions

In a mixing bowl

Add chopped garlic, olive oil, freshly ground black pepper, salt, chopped coriander if like and mix well.

Using a sharp knife, pin holes into steaks and stuff in holes some chopped garlic. Grate meats onto garlic mixture and put steaks in packet or cover the bowl with a foil. Then place in refrigerator for 4 hours.

Preheat air fryer for 5 minutes at 200°C or 390°F

Fry for 5 minutes at 200°C or 390°F and then turn stakes, reduce the temperature and fry for another 5 minutes at 180°C or 360°F.

After 10 minutes at all take the steak out of the air fryer and place it on a plate.

Let steaks cool down for another 3 minutes.

Done.

## Veal Sage Meat

*Prep Time 10 min+30 min marinate//Cook Time 5 minutes*

*Servings 4//Temp 205ºC or 400ºF//No Skill Requires*

### Ingredients

1 lb. of veal tenderloin

1 tbsp. of sage leaves, fresh chopped

2 cloves of garlic peeled and chopped

1 teaspoon of olive oil

1/4 teaspoon of black pepper freshly ground

1/4 teaspoon of salt

## Directions

In a mixing bowl

Add chopped garlic, olive oil, freshly ground black pepper, salt, chopped sage leaves and mix well.

Grate meats onto garlic mixture and put steaks in packet or cover the bowl with a foil. Take aside for 30 minutes.

Fry for 3 minutes at 205ºC or 400ºF and then turn stakes, and fry for another 2 minutes at 205ºC or 400ºF.

After 5 minutes at all take the steak out of the air fryer and place it on a plate.

Let steaks rest for another 1 minute.

## Wine Beef Steaks

*Prep Time 10 min+1 hour marinate // Cook Time 30 minutes*
*Servings 4//Temp 180-200ºC or 360-390ºF//Requires Minimum Skill*

## Ingredients

4 beef steaks about 5 oz. each one

2 oz. of soy sauce

2 oz. of rice cooking wine

1 tablespoons white sugar

1 tablespoons minced garlic

1 teaspoon of sesame oil

¼ teaspoon of black pepper freshly ground

½ teaspoon hot chilli paste

¼ teaspoon of salt

## Directions

### *In a mixing bowl*

Add soy sauce, rice wine, sugar, garlic, sesame oil, pepper, chilli paste and salt then mix well.

Pour 1/2 of this mixture over the beef and marinate at least one hour at room temperature, or longer in the refrigerator.

Preheat air fryer for 5 minutes at 180ºC or 360ºF

Fry for 5 minutes at 180ºC or 360ºF and then turn stakes and fry for another 5 minutes at 180ºC or 360ºF.

After 10 minutes at all take the steak out of the air fryer and place it on a plate.

Let steaks rest for another 3 minutes.

# CHAPTER THREE SEAFOOD RECIPES

## Crispy Rice Spicy Tuna Sushi

*Prep Time 30 minutes // Cook Time: 15 minutes*

*Servings 2 // Temp 200ºC or 390ºF // Requires Specific Skill*

## Ingredients

½ lbs. tuna

1 ½ cups cooked sushi rice

3 tablespoons of vinegar

1 teaspoon of sugar

2-3 green onions stalk

2 teaspoons of soy sauce

1 teaspoon of siracha sauce

Olive oil

## Directions

### Make the sushi rice first

Rinse the 1 ½ cup of rice in a colander or strainer until the water runs clear and put in a thick-bottomed pan, pour 15.5 fl.oz. (450 ml) of water. The pan should be filled with water and rice no more than a third. Cover the pan with a lid, turn on the medium heat, bring to a boil, and then lower the heat to a minimum, boil the rice lightly for 10-15 minutes until the water is completely absorbed, remove the pan from the stove without opening the lid for another 10-15 minutes.

Pour into the empty cup 3 tablespoons of vinegar,

Add 1 teaspoon of sugar into vinegar and mix it up thoroughly,

Add the vinegar mixture into rice and mix vinegar into rice.

### Make the spicy tuna topping now

Slice then dice tuna into small chunks.

Chopped green onions into very fine pieces then add green onion into tuna.

Add 2 teaspoons of soy sauce

Add 1 teaspoon of siracha sauce

Mix everything up thoroughly.

### Mold the nigiri rice

Add plastic wrap on top of the bamboo sheet.

Add rice on the sheet and covered all rice surface with plastic wrap.

Then roll squeeze rice with bamboo sheet.

Shape and make sure rice is tightly stacked together.

Wet hand and knife, then cut them into evenly chunks.

Wet fingers and tighten each rice chunks again.

Spray olive oil on rice chunks.

Fry nigiri rice for 13 minutes at 200ºC *or 390ºF*

Add toppings on nigiri rice.

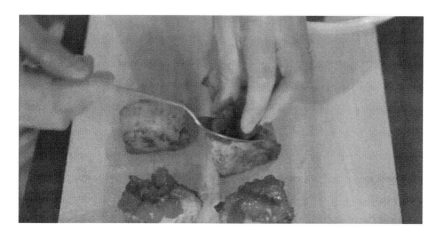

*Tip: for every 7 oz. (200 grams) of rice should be 8.5 fl.oz. (250 ml) of water.*

*For the aroma in rice put a square of seaweed nori (Kombu), but it must necessarily have time to remove before boiling water.*

# Codfish Pancake.

*Prep Time 15 minutes // Cook Time 7 minutes*

*Servings 4//Temp 190°C or 375°F/Requires Minimum Skill*

## Ingredients

2 lbs. cod fish

4 green onions

2 garlic gloves

2 chilies peppers

3 eggs

1 pinch of salt and pepper

1 tsp. of <u>light soy sauce</u>

½ cup of flour

## Directions

Chop up 4 green onions,

Slice 2 garlic gloves,

Chop up 2 chilies peppers,

Whisk 3 eggs and whisk in chilies, green onion and garlic,

Add 1 pinch of salt and pepper,

Add a teaspoon of light soy sauce and mix well.

Take skin off cod and cut cod into regular shapes,

Add ½ cup of flour into cod and wrap the pieces of fish in the flour, then dip floured cod into egg mix.

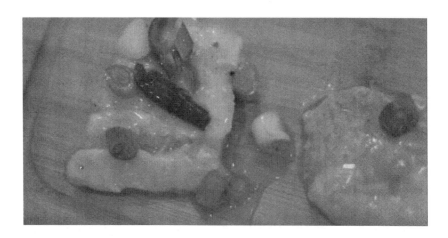

Place cod filets on the basket,
Air fry cod for 7 minutes at 190ºC or 375ºF

*Tip: add a piece of parchment paper into the air fryer tray and the egg mix will not drip down.*

# Crab Rissole

*Prep Time 10 minutes // Cook Time 15 minutes*
*Servings 4 // Temp 180°C or 360°F // Requires Minimum Skill*

## Ingredients

1 lb. of crabmeat

1 egg, beaten

½ cup of panko Japanese breadcrumbs

¼ cup of light mayonnaise

2 tablespoons of chives, minced

1 tablespoon of Dijon mustard

1 tablespoon of lemon juice

1 teaspoon of celery seed

1 teaspoon of onion powder

¼ teaspoon of pepper, freshly ground

1 tablespoon of chili sauce

1 tablespoon of extra-virgin olive oil

## Directions

### *In mixing bowl*

Add crabmeat, bread crumbs, chives, onion powder, celery seeds salt and pepper and mix well with hands or using spatula.

### *In second mixing bowl*

Add egg, mayonnaise, Dijon mustard, lemon juice, hot sauce and oil, then beat well using whisk or fork.

Add the contents of the second bowl into the crab mince and mix well with hands.

Form into 4 patties and place on a baking sheet.

Preheat air fryer for 3 minutes at 180°C or 360°F

Place inside air fryer basket a baking sheet and put patties on sheet.

Fry for 10 minutes at 180°C or 360°F

If you want more fried rissole, then fry for further 5 minutes at 180°C or 360°F

# Crumbed Salmon

*Prep Time 10 minutes // Cook Time 12 minutes*

*Servings 3//Temp 180°C or 360°F//Requires Minimum Skill*

## Ingredients

3 salmon fillets

4 oz. of panko breadcrumbs

3 tablespoons of vegetable oil

1/4 teaspoon of thyme powder

1/8 teaspoon of sea salt fine

1 egg whisked

1 lemon sliced to serve

## Directions

### *In a mixing bowl*

Add oil, breadcrumbs, thyme and salt then mix until the mixture gets loose and crumbly.

### *Into plate* add beaten egg.

Dip the salmon fillets into the egg then shake off any rest. Dip the fillets into the panko mixture and sprinkle until evenly and fully coated.

Preheat air fryer for 5 minutes at 180°C or 360°F

Put into the basket panko fish fillets and fry for 12 minutes at 180°C or 360°F.

Serve immediately with lemon.

# Delicious Japanese Panko Shrimps

*Prep Time 20 minutes // Cook Time 10 minutes*

*Servings 2 // Temp 180ºC or 360ºF //Requires Specific Skill*

## Ingredients

12 oz. of tiger shrimp

2 tablespoon of <u>corn starch</u>

2 eggs

1/3 cup of <u>all-purpose flour</u>

¾ teaspoon of salt

½ teaspoon of black pepper

1 cup of <u>Kikkoman Japanese-style panko breadcrumbs</u>

## Directions

Peel and rinse tiger shrimp.

Drain shrimp and add corn starch. Give it a mix.

Add a bit of water and keep mixing (this gets rid of the fishy smell and keeps the shrimp tender).

Leave that soak about 5 minutes, and let's prepare the breading.


Beat 2 eggs together (add a bit of water).

Mix salt and pepper together with the flour.


Rinse the shrimp and dry with paper towels,

Transfer the shrimp onto a dry plate.

Cut slits along the underbelly of the shrimp (so they doesn't curl when heated)


## Prepare the panko:

First roll the shrimp in the flour,

Then dunk it into the egg mixture,

Finally smother it in panko.


Put the breaded shrimps into the air fryer and fry for 10 minutes at 180ºC or 360ºF

# Fire Pepper Chilli Prawns.

*Prep Time 15 minutes // Cook Time 6 minutes*

*Servings 1//Temp 200ºC or 390ºF//Requires Minimum Skill*

## Ingredients

12 oz. small prawns

2 teaspoons of beaten egg

1 teaspoon of green chilies, finely chopped

½ teaspoon of garlic, finely chopped

½ teaspoon of pepper powder

½ teaspoon of red chilli paste

1 teaspoon of cornstarch

1 teaspoon of all-purpose flour

¼ teaspoon of soya sauce

½ teaspoon of green chilli sauce

1 ½ teaspoon of lemon juice

1 pinch of sugar

1 teaspoon of vinegar

## Directions

In a mixing bowl, add in the small variety of prawns, beaten egg, green chilies, garlic, pepper powder, red chili paste, cornstarch, all- purpose flour, soya sauce, green chili sauce, sugar, vinegar, salt, and lemon juice. Mix all ingredients well.

In a plate, put some breadcrumbs. Dip the spice coated prawns in the breadcrumbs. Do it fine, so that they get coated well.

Preheat the air fryer at 200°C or 390°F for 3 minutes.

Put the prawn pieces into the basket and fry them at 200°C or 390°F for 3 minutes.

After 3 minutes, open the air fryer, spray the prawn pieces with little oil and again fry for another 3 minutes.

*Tip: Shake off excessive breading using a sieve with a handle*

## Fried Salmon

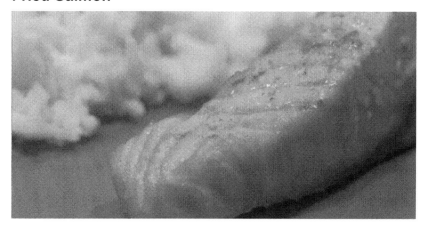

*Prep Time 10 minutes // Cook Time 7 minutes*

*Servings 4//Temp 130ºC or 260ºF//No Skill Requires*

## Ingredients

4 slices of Salmon

¼ teaspoon of sea salt fine

2 teaspoons of lime juice (½ tsp. for each fish slice)

2 teaspoons of olive oil

½ teaspoon of white pepper crushed

Spring of rosemary

## Directions

Season the salmon with salt, lime juice, oil, and pepper.

Put fish in the air fryer with the skin on the basket and place fresh rosemary on top.

Fry for 10 minutes at 130ºC or 260ºF

If you want more golden brown, fry for another 3-5 minutes.

# King Fish Asian Fry Style

*Prep Time 20 minutes // Cook Time 7 minutes*

*Servings 4 // Temp 180ºC or 360ºF // Requires Specific Skill*

## Ingredients

2 lb. of King Fish (8-10 pieces)

Salt at taste

Juice of one lime

½ teaspoon of ginger, finely chopped

½ teaspoon of garlic, finely chopped

½ teaspoon of chilli flakes (optional)

¼ teaspoon of ajwain seeds

½ teaspoon of pepper powder

½ cup of chickpea flour

Juice of half lemon

¼ teaspoon of Haldi powder

Soak <u>wooden skewer</u> in water for 15 minutes

## Directions

### *In a mixing bowl*

Add in finely chopped ginger, garlic, ajwain seeds, green chilies, chilli flakes, pepper powder, chickpea flour, lemon juice, turmeric powder and bit of water.

Mix well to get a thick batter.

Marinade the King Fish pieces with few salt and lemon juices, mix it and put aside for 10 – 15 minutes.

Take the fish pieces and mix them well in a mess in mixing bowl until the pieces will be coated well.

Preheat the air fryer for 3 minutes at 180°C or 360°F

Take a wooden skewer and run them through the fish pieces. Put 2 fish pieces on each skewer.

Carefully place the skewers into air fryer basket.

Fry the fish pieces for about 7-8 minutes at 180°C or 360°F.

*Tip: After 4 minutes, pull out the basket and spray or brush the pieces with little oil and close.*

## Spicy Chinese Prawns

*Prep Time 20 minutes // Cook Time 7 minutes*

*Servings 1 // Temp 180°C or 360°F // Requires Specific Skill*

## Ingredients

10 oz. of prawns

1 teaspoon of corn flour

1 pinch of sugar

1 teaspoon of vinegar

½ teaspoon of garlic chopped

½ teaspoon of ginger chopped

½ teaspoons of soya sauce

1 Pinch of MSG (Monosodium glutamate)

½ teaspoon of chilli flakes

1 teaspoon of chilli sauce

1 teaspoon of butter

2 tablespoon of bread crumbs

1 sheet of spring roll wrappers

## Directions

### *In a bowl*

Add prawns, corn flour, sugar, vinegar, chopped garlic & ginger, soya sauce, MSG, chilli flakes, chili sauce *(All ingredients, except the last three)*

Mix it and coat the prawns well.

### *On a table*

Apply the butter on spring roll sheet top,

Then sprinkle some breadcrumbs and cut sheet into thin strips.

Take the strips and roll up the prawns well.

Preheat air fryer for 2 minutes at 180°C or 360°F.

Put the prepared prawns in the air fryer and fry them for 7 minutes at 180°C or 360°F

## White Fish Sticks

*Prep Time 20 minutes // Cook Time 8 minutes*

*Servings 2 // Temp 180°C or 360⁰F // Requires Specific Skill*

## Ingredients

1 lb. of fresh White Fish fillets, skinned and boned

4 oz. of whole meal bread crumbs

2 oz. of all-purpose flour

1 Medium Egg beaten

1 Small Lemon, juice

1 teaspoon of parsley

1 teaspoon of thyme

½ teaspoon of oregano

½ teaspoon of marjoram

Pinch of salt

Pinch of pepper

## Directions

### *In food processor*

Add fish filet, lemon juice, salt and pepper, thyme, oregano and marjoram. When all mashed like uncooked fishcakes, you can get start making fish sticks.

### *In a mixing bowl*

Add breadcrumbs, salt & pepper, parsley and mix well.

### *Into plate*

Add beaten egg.

### *Into another plate*

Add all-purpose flour.

Coat fish pieces in the flour, then coat in the egg and finish this with rolling it in the breadcrumbs.

Put the Fish sticks in the basket and fry them for 8 minutes at 180°C or 360°F

Serve with potatoes and <u>tartar sauce</u> or onto a sandwich.

# CHAPTER FOUR POULTRY RECIPES

## Buffalo Chicken Wings

*Prep Time 10 minutes // Cook Time: 25 minutes*

*Servings 4 // Temp 180ºC or 360ºF // No Skill Requires*

### Ingredients

2 lbs. chicken wings

1 cup of <u>self raising flour</u>

4 oz. real butter

<u>Franks Red Hot Sauce</u>

### Directions

Preheat air fryer 2 minutes at 180°C or 360°F.

Cut tip of wing and discard cut at the center joint to create 2 pieces.

Coat the wings with the self raising flour.

Add the wings to the basket and shake well.

Place basket in air fryer for 25 minutes at 180°C or 360°F,

Remove basket every 5 minutes and shake.

After 25 minutes they will be Golden Brown, but give them 10 more minutes if you like them nice and crispy.

## Make the sauce

You will need Franks Red Hot Sauce and butter.

Melt the butter in saucepan over a medium heat,

Once butter melted mix with a Franks Red Hot Sauce.

Remove wings from air fryer and mix with sauce.

# Cayenne Chicken Wings

*Prep Time 10 minutes // Cook Time 25 minutes*
*Servings 2//Temp 180-200ºC or 360-390ºF//No Skill Requires*

## Ingredients

8 – 10 pcs. of chicken wings
½ cup of natural yogurt
½ teaspoon of cayenne (chilli) powder
½ teaspoon of garlic, finely chopped
¼ teaspoon of oregano
¼ teaspoon of dry parsley
1 teaspoon of oil
½ tablespoon of vinegar
¼ teaspoon of black pepper, freshly crushed
Salt to taste

## Directions

### In a mixing bowl

Add yogurt, cayenne powder, finely chopped garlic, oregano, dry parsley and mix well.

Coat chicken wings well with the marinade. Put in the refrigerator for about 3-4 hours. But if you need it quickly you can start cooking them right away.

Before frying add little vinegar, oil, freshly crushed pepper in bowl with marinated wings and mix all well.

Preheat the AirFryer for 3 minutes at 200°C or 390°F

Put the chicken wings in basket and fry for 3-4 minutes at 200°C or 390°F

After 3-4 minutes, lower the temperature to 180°C or 360°F and fry for 2-3 minutes more.

# Chicken Lollipops.

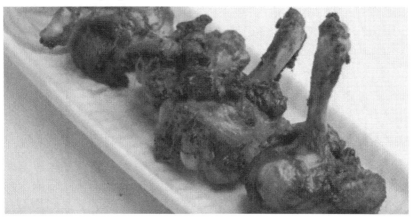

*Prep Time 20 minutes // Cook Time 9 minutes*

*Servings 2 // Temp 180ºC or 360⁰F // Requires Specific Skill*

## Ingredients

10 oz. of chicken wings (only drumette parts of wings)
½ teaspoon of soya sauce
½ of egg
1 teaspoon of chili paste
1 teaspoon of vinegar
1 teaspoon of chili powder
½ teaspoon of ginger garlic paste
½ bunch of coriander chopped
½ teaspoon pepper powder
½ teaspoon of garlic chopped
Cornstarch
1 tablespoon of all-purpose flour
½ teaspoon of salt
2 teaspoons of lime juice
2 tablespoons of oil

## Directions

### In a bowl

Add soya sauce, egg mixture, chili paste, vinegar, chili powder, ginger garlic paste, chopped coriander, pepper powder, chopped garlic and mix it well.

Add chicken wings, cornstarch, all-purpose flour, lime juice mix it well again.

Preheat the air fryer for 3 minutes at 180°C or 360°F

Place the chicken wings in the basket and fry them for 5 minutes at 180°C or 360°F

After 5 minutes pull them out and spray the oil and again put them back into the Air Fryer and fry them for 4 minutes at 180°C or 360°F

Enjoy!

*Tip: Cut with a knife in the area of the joint and then, pull the meat down with your hand. Hold the bone with your other hand.*

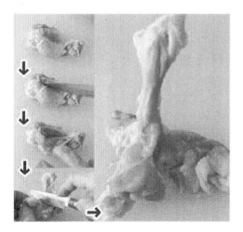

## Chicken Yakitori Sticks.

*Prep Time 10 minutes // Cook Time 10 minutes*

*Servings 2 // Temp 180°C or 360°F//Requires Minimum Skill*

### Ingredients

1 ½ lbs. boneless, skinless chicken breast

3 big green onions stalk

¼ cup of <u>soy sauce</u>

1 tsp. of sugar

1 tbsp. of <u>mirin</u>

1 tsp. of <u>garlic salt</u>

### Directions

Soak <u>bamboo sticks</u> in water for 15 minutes

Cut chicken into 1 inch square pieces

Cut green onions into 1 inch length

Add chicken and onion into skewer sticks

Alternate chicken and green onion in bamboo sticks

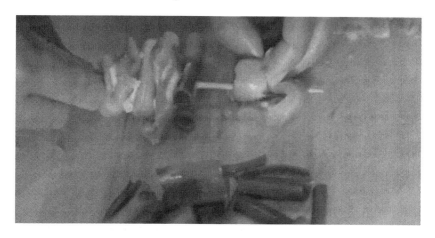

**Make the marinade**

Add ¼ cup of soy sauce

Add 1 teaspoon of sugar

Add 1 tablespoon of mirin

Add 1 teaspoon of garlic salt

Stir the sauce until it's evenly mixed.

Add marinade into chicken and let it marinade for a few hours.

Fry skewers for 8 to 10 minutes at 180ºC or 360ºF

**Crispy Duck Legs.**

*Prep Time 5 minutes // Cook Time 30 minutes*

*Servings 2//Temp 175-200ºC or 350-390ºF//No Skill Requires*

**Ingredients**

2 duck legs

1 tsp of <u>five spice powder</u>

½ tbsp of chopped parsley

½ tbsp of chopped thyme

½ tbsp of salt and pepper

**Directions**

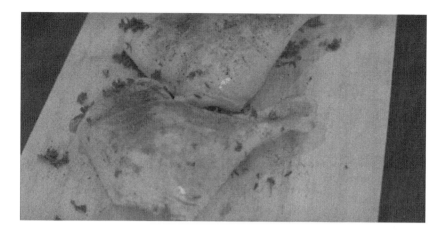

Rub spices & herbs all over duck legs.

Fry them 25 minutes in 170° C or 350° F.

Fry them for another 5 minutes in 200° C or 390° F.


Done and enjoy!

# Crispy Chicken Dumplings

*Prep Time 30 minutes // Cook Time 10 minutes*

*Servings 1 // Temp 180°C or 360°F// Requires Specific Skill*

## Ingredients

1 cup of all-purpose flour

1 pinch of salt

8 oz. of chicken mince

One Egg, beaten

1 teaspoon of white or spring onion, finely chopped

1 teaspoon of green onion, finely chopped

1 tablespoon of French beans, finely chopped

1 tablespoon of carrot, finely chopped

1 tablespoon of coriander leaves, finely chopped

½ teaspoon of green chilies, finely chopped

½ teaspoon of pepper powder

¼ of soya sauce

½ of cornstarch

1 teaspoon of sesame seed oil


**Dough for the outer casing:**

*In a mixing bowl,*

Add all-purpose flour, a pinch of salt and by a little hot water,

Knead to make stiff dough.

Cover and keep aside.

Also, you can take puff pastry to your taste.


**For the filling**

*In another mixing bowl,*

Add chicken pieces, egg, white or spring onion, green onion, French beans, carrots, green chilies, coriander leaves, pepper powder, soya sauce, cornstarch and mix well.

Add some sesame seed oil and mix again.

Keep aside.


*On a table or Pastry Mat,*

With help of <u>rolling pin</u>, fug some flour on the table and roll the dough into a thin sheet. Take a <u>round cookie cutter</u> and cut into roundels about 4" in full and keep aside.

Use some water on the edges of the dough round. Take some stuffing and place in the round and press the edges (half-moon shape).

Preheat the Air fryer for 4 minutes at 180°C or 360°F

Spray or brush the dumplings with little oil.

Put dumplings in Air fryer and fry for 7 minutes at 180°C or 360°F

Then, remove and turn the dumplings and fry again for about 3-4 minutes at 180°C or 360°F

You can spray some oil on dumplings top if need.

Serve with favorite sauce.

# Fried Chicken Cutlet

*Prep Time 10 minutes // Cook Time 25 minutes*

*Servings 2 // Temp 180°C or 360°F // Requires Specific Skill*

## Ingredients

1 cup of flour

1 cup of panko breadcrumbs

2 pinches of salt and pepper

4 pieces of boneless chicken thigh meat

1 Egg

2 sprays of olive oil

## Directions

Add salt and pepper into the flour,

Stir salt and pepper in the flour bowl.

Also add salt and pepper into the panko bowl.

Coat chicken in flour,

Then coat chicken in egg,

Then coat chicken in panko.

Add them into the Air fryer,

Spray olive oil onto the chicken.

Fry it for 20 minutes at 180°C or 360°F,

Then fry it for 5 minutes at 200° C or 390° F for extra crispy texture

## Make the sauce

If you don't have a favorite sauce, here's a simple recipe you can make.

Pour into the small saucepan:

1 tablespoon of soy sauce,

Add 1 teaspoon of sesame oil,

Add 1 teaspoon of garlic salt,

Add 1 teaspoon of sugar,

Add 1 teaspoon of rice vinegar.

Stir until everything is mixed in.

# Hush Puppy Chicken

*Prep Time 20 minutes // Cook Time 8 minutes*
*Servings 3 // Temp 180ºC or 360ºF // No Skill Requires*

## Ingredients

4 oz. of corn meal flour

4 oz. of all-purpose flour

½ teaspoon of baking powder

¼ teaspoon of baking soda

Salt to taste

1 tablespoon of butter

5 oz. of chicken, finely chopped

1 teaspoon of garlic, finely chopped

One medium onion, finely chopped

1 teaspoon of pepper powder, freshly crushed

1 tablespoon of coriander leaves, finely chopped

3.5 fl. oz. of water

7 fl. oz. of milk

1 teaspoon of sugar

1 teaspoon of oil

## Directions

### *In a mixing bowl*

Add cornmeal flour, all-purpose flour, baking powder, baking soda, and salt.

Mix all ingredients using spoon and keep aside.

### *Heat a small saucepan*

Add a tablespoon of butter,

When butter melts, add chicken pieces and let it start fried,

As soon as the chicken begins to be roasted add garlic and onion,

Keep frying sometimes stirring with spatula the chicken should be lightly fried with onions,

Add crushed pepper and coriander leaves, and mix well.

Then add water and milk, mix all ingredients and let it boil.

Add salt to taste and little sugar and mix well.

Once it starts boiling, switch off the flame and add the flour mixture, mix it with spatula to make dough.

### *In a big bowl*

Pour out of the saucepan preparing dough mix into a big bowl,

Add beaten eggs and mix well with spatula or spoon.

Dust some flour in your fingers and shape dough into balls about 1.5 - 2" around, and keep aside.

Coat the balls with brush or oil sprayer of 1 teaspoon of oil.

Preheat the Air fryer for 3 minutes at 180°C or 360°F

Fry for 8 minutes at 180°C or 360°F

Serve with favorite sauce.

## Roast Chicken and Potatoes

*Prep Time 5 minutes // Cook Time 35 minutes*

*Servings 3 // Temp 200ºC or 390ºF // No Skill Requires*

## Ingredients

2 – 3 lbs. fresh chicken

6 medium potatoes

1 tablespoon of olive oil

2 teaspoon of <u>Spices for chicken</u> to taste

1 teaspoon of salt

½ teaspoon of pepper

**Directions**

Preheat Air fryer for 2 minutes at 200°C or 390°F.

Sprinkle chicken with salt, pepper and chicken spice.

Put chicken into Air fryer for 35 minutes at 200° C or 390° F

Peel and wash potatoes and spray them with oil.

Potatoes need to be added to cook for at least 25 minutes.

*Tip: Chicken can be marinated or filled with stuffing if desired.*

# Sausage Stuffed in Chicken Filet

*Prep Time 15 minutes // Cook Time 15 minutes*

*Servings 4 // Temp 190ºC or 375ºF // Requires Specific Skill*

## Ingredients

4 sausage

2 lbs. tenderize chicken meat

1 pinch of salt and pepper

Spices for chicken to taste

8 toothpicks

## Directions

Roll to tenderize chicken meat with a rolling pin,

Add 1 pinch of salt and pepper. You can also add spices for chicken to taste.

Remove sausage casing with a knife.

Place sausage meat onto chicken filet, and then roll it,

Seal filet by threading filets with 2 toothpicks.

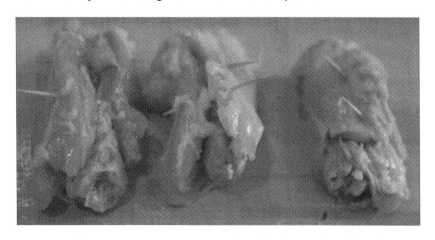

Place chicken into the Air fryer tray,

Fry meat for 15 minutes at 190° C or 375° F

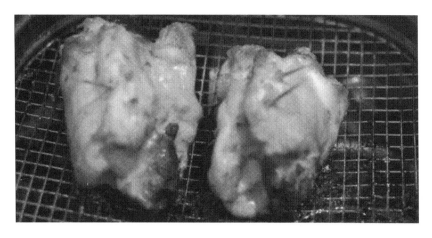

# Spicy Chicken Wings

*Prep Time 10 minutes // Cook Time 10 minutes*

*Servings 4//Temp 180°C or 360°F//Requires Minimum Skill*

## Ingredients

8 - 10 pcs. of chicken wings, with skin

### For the marinade:

1 teaspoon of garlic, chopped

1 tablespoon of soya sauce

½ teaspoon of oregano

1 tablespoon of lemon juice

½ teaspoon of black pepper, crushed

Salt to taste

### For the Sauce:

2 teaspoons of spring onions, finely chopped

1 tablespoon of vinegar

1 teaspoon of brown sugar

1 tablespoon of tomato ketchup

1 tablespoon of chili sauce

## Directions

### *In a mixing bowl marinade the wings*

Add finely chopped garlic, soya sauce, oregano, lemon juice, salt and freshly crushed black pepper. Mix this marinade well.

Add the chicken wings to the marinade and coat it well. Place the marinated chicken wings in the refrigerator for at least 2 hours.

After two hours, remove the wings from the refrigerator.

Strew some flour on chicken wings and mix well. Repeat this for about 2 to 3 times. (This will help in giving a nice texture to the chicken wings when frying.)

### *In medium bowl prepare the sauce*

Add finely chopped spring onions, vinegar, brown sugar and mix well until the sugar melts.

Add tomato ketchup, chili sauce and mix well.


Preheat the Air fryer for 3 minutes at 180°C or 360°F

Put in Air fryer basket the marinated chicken wings and fry for 3 minutes at 180°C or 360°F

Then, remove the basket and turn over the wings and fry it for another 3 minutes at 180°C or 360°F

After 6 minutes in total, open the Air fryer tray and grease the chicken wings with the sauce and fry them again for 2 to 3 minutes at 180°C or 360°F

# CHAPTER _ BURGERS and SANDWICHES RECIPES

## Avocado Whopper Burger King

*Prep Time 10 minutes // Cook Time 10 minutes*

*Servings 4//Temp 180°C or 360°F//Requires Minimum Skill*

### Ingredients

14 oz. of low-fat minced pork

4 whole meal burger buns

1 small avocado

1 small onion, peeled and diced

2 tablespoons of spring onion

Salad Garnish

Tomato and cucumber, sliced

1 tablespoon of Worcester sauce

1 tablespoon of tomato ketchup

1 teaspoon garlic puree

1/4 teaspoon of basil

1/4 teaspoon of oregano

1 teaspoon of thyme

1 teaspoon of parsley

1/8 teaspoon of salt

1/4 teaspoon of pepper

Avocado Sauce

**Ingredients for Avocado Sauce**

1 garlic clove

2 medium Avocados

1 teaspoon of chives

1 lime juice & rind

7 fl.oz. of Coconut milk

Pinch of salt & pepper


**Directions**

**In a mixing bowl**

Add mince, diced onion, Worcester sauce, ketchup,
1 tsp. of garlic puree,
¼ tsp. of basil,
¼ tsp. of oregano,
1 tsp. of thyme,
1 tsp. of parsley,
1/8 tsp. of salt,
¼ tsp. of pepper,
½ of Avocado and
1 tbsp. of spring onion,
And mix well with your hands until smooth.

Make mince into burgers and place in the fridge for 10 minutes.

Preheat Air fryer for 3 minutes at 180°C or 360°F

Put into Air fryer basket a baking sheet and put burgers on sheet.

Fry for 10 minutes at 180°C or 360°F

Put salad garnish on the bottom of a burger bun, then add the burger, grease with avocado sauce, sliced avocado, sliced tomato and cucumber. Place the bun on the burger and serve.

*Tip Time may vary in the range of 8 - 12 minutes, depending on the thickness of your burger.*

### Make an Avocado Sauce

Peel and dice the garlic and put it in the soup maker,

Add fresh of avocados it to the soup maker,

Add 1 tsp Chives, 7 fl.oz. of Coconut milk, lime juice & rind, salt&pepper,

Blend all ingredients in the soup maker.

Done.

# Crispy Salmon Burger

*Prep Time 10 minutes // Cook Time 12 minutes*
*Servings 4 // Temp 180°C or 360°F // Requires Specific Skill*

## Ingredients

3 (7.5 oz. each one) cans of salmon

2 oz. of minced celery

2 oz. of Tartar sauce

1 cup plain dried bread crumbs,

4 scallions

1/4 teaspoon of dried thyme

2 large eggs

1/4 cup of olive oil

4 burger buns

2 oz. of Tartar sauce and salad leaves, for serving

## Directions

*In mixing bowl*

Drain salmon, remove bones and skin and put meat in a bowl. Mash fish with a fork.

Add 2 oz. celery, 2 oz. Tartar sauce, and 2 tbsp. of breadcrumbs,

Add two finely chopped scallions and mix well with hands or using spatula.

### In second mixing bowl

Add remaining breadcrumbs (about 3/4 cup),

Add two finely chopped scallion greens and thyme, and then combine it.

### In third bowl, beat eggs well.

Form salmon mixture into 4 patties.

Coat patties in bread crumbs, turn in beaten egg, then coat in bread crumbs again and place on a baking sheet.

Preheat Air fryer for 3 minutes at 180°C or 360°F

Place inside Air fryer basket a baking sheet and put salmon burgers on sheet.

Fry for 7 minutes at 180°C or 360°F

If you want more fried burgers, then fry for further 5 minutes at 180°C or 360°F

Spread some tartar sauce at the bottom of the bun and place Lettuce leaf, then using tongs place a salmon burger. Onto burger spread some tartar sauce, and then press the other bun on top.

Repeat this with all burgers.

Serve with fry potatoes and Tartar sauce.

# Double Cheese Burger

*Prep Time 10 minutes // Cook Time 11 minutes*
*Servings 2//Temp 180°C or 360°F//Requires Minimum Skill*

## Ingredients

2 burger buns

10 oz. of pork mince

½ of onion finely diced

½ of small onion peeled and sliced

4 oz. of Cheddar cheese

1/2 tablespoon of soft cheese

Pinch of salt

Pinch of pepper

## Directions

### In a mixing bowl

Add the mince, the diced onion, salt and pepper, the soft cheese and mix well with hands or spatula so that all ingredients are well mixed.

Then divide the meat mix into 4 even sized burgers.


Preheat Air Fryer for 3 minutes at 180°C or 360°F

Place inside Air fryer basket a baking sheet and put burgers on sheet.

Fry for 9 minutes at 180°C or 360°F

Open the Air fryer basket and sprinkle soft cheese on top.

After that fry for another 2 minutes at 160°C or 320°F


When the burgers frying are about 5 minutes, place the sliced onion in saucepan with a little olive oil and allow to sauté.


Place salad garnishes at the bottom of the bun then put a burger.

Between the burgers put a slice of cheese and some sliced onion, and then press the other bun on top.

Sprinkle with some more cheese along with some fried onion.

Also, you can put another slice of cheese on second meat top.

## Easy Crab Burger

*Prep Time 10 minutes // Cook Time 15 minutes*
*Servings 4 // Temp 180°C or 360°F // Requires Specific Skill*

**Ingredients**

1 lb. of crabmeat

1 egg, beaten

½ cup of panko Japanese breadcrumbs

¼ cup of light mayonnaise

2 tablespoons of chives, minced

1 tablespoon of Dijon mustard

1 tablespoon of lemon juice

1 teaspoon of celery seed

1 teaspoon of onion powder

¼ teaspoon of pepper, freshly ground

1 tablespoon of chili sauce

4 oz. of Tartar sauce

1 tablespoon of extra-virgin olive oil

2 teaspoons of butter

2 burger buns

2 Lettuce leafs

## Directions

### In mixing bowl

Add crabmeat, bread crumbs, chives, onion powder, celery seeds salt and pepper and mix well with hands or using spatula.

### In second mixing bowl

Add egg, mayonnaise, Dijon mustard, lemon juice, hot sauce, oil and butter, then beat well using whisk or fork.

Add the contents of the second bowl into the crab mince and mix well with hands.

Form into 4 patties and place on a baking sheet.

Preheat Air fryer for 3 minutes at 180°C or 360°F

Place inside Air Fryer basket a baking sheet and put burgers on sheet.

Fry for 10 minutes at 180°C or 360°F

If you want more fried burgers, then fry for further 5 minutes at 180°C or 360°F

Spread some Tartar sauce at the bottom of the bun and place Lettuce leaf, then using tongs place a crab burger. Onto burger spread some Tartar sauce, and then press the other bun on top.

Repeat this with all burgers.

# Juicy Burger with Pickled Red Onion

*Prep Time 10 minutes // Cook Time 20 minutes*

*Servings 4 // Temp 180°C or 360°F // Requires Specific Skill*

## Ingredients

2 burger buns
10 oz. of ground beef
1 small onion, diced into small pieces
1 medium cucumber, sliced
2 Lettuce leafs
2 tablespoons of Worcestershire sauce
1 cloves garlic, diced into small pieces
1/4 cup of breadcrumbs
1/8 teaspoon of cayenne pepper
1 egg
1/8 teaspoon of salt
Pinch of pepper

## *Pickled onion*

1 medium red onion, sliced into thin rings
1/2 cups of apple cider vinegar
1 tablespoon of sugar

1 cup of water, room temperature.

## Directions

### *In a mixing bowl*

Add the mince, the diced onion and garlic, salt and pepper, Worcestershire sauce and cayenne pepper, breadcrumbs and egg, and mix well with hands or spatula so that all ingredients are well mixed.

Then divide the meat mix into 2 even sized burgers.

Preheat Air fryer for 3 minutes at 180°C or 360°F

Place inside Air fryer basket a baking sheet and put burgers on sheet.

Fry for 15 minutes at 180°C or 360°F

If you want more fried meat, then cook burgers for further 5-10 minutes at 180°C or 360°F

When the burgers frying are about 5 minutes, place the sliced red onion in saucepan with a cup of water, ½ cup of apple cider vinegar, 1 tbsp. of sugar and allow onion to marinate about 10 minutes. Dry the onions using paper towels.

Place Lettuce leaf at the bottom of the bun and put two slices of pickled onion, then using a tongs place a burger. Onto burger put some slices of pickled onion and sliced cucumber, then press the other bun on top.

## The Ultimate Burger

*Prep Time 10 minutes // Cook Time 40 minutes*
*Servings 4 // Temp 200°C or 390°F // Requires Specific Skill*

## Ingredients

12 oz. of mixed pork&beef mince or 6 oz. mince pork and 6 oz. mince beef

1 medium onion

1 teaspoon of garlic puree

1 teaspoon of tomato puree

1 teaspoon of mustard

1 teaspoon of basil

¼ teaspoon of marjoram

¼ teaspoon of oregano

¼ teaspoon of thyme

¼ teaspoon of salt

¼ teaspoon of pepper

1 oz. of cheddar cheese

4 Bread Buns

Salad for burger topping

## Directions

### *In a mixing bowl*

Add the mince and all rest ingredients and mix well.

Form into four medium-sized burgers and spray little oil on ready-to-cook food.

Spray oil in the Air Fryer basket and put burgers inside.

Fry in the Air Fryer for 25 minutes at 200°C or 390°F and then check the burgers. If you want more fried meat, then cook burgers for further 15 minutes at 180°C or 360°F

Add salad, cheese, fried patties on bun and serve.

# Cheesy Prosciutto Sandwich.

## Cheesy sandwich with Prosciutto, Mozzarella, Tomato and Basil

*Prep Time: 5 minutes // Cook Time: 5 minutes*

*Servings: 1 // Temp: 200° C or 390° F // No Skill Requires*

## Ingredients

2 - 3 slices of bread

4 oz. of prosciutto

2 oz. of mozzarella cheese

Olive Oil

One tomato

Salt and Pepper

Basil leaves

## Directions

Lay out 2 slices of bread

Add prosciutto on piece of bread

Add mozzarella cheese on prosciutto

Cover the top with a second piece of bread

Place into an Air fryer

Fry for 5 minutes at 200° C or 390° F

Remove from Air fryer with a spatula

Sprinkle olive oil on top

Season with salt and pepper

Add tomato slices on top of a second piece of bread

Add basil leaves.

Cover the third with a piece of bread at will.

# Simple Burger

*Prep Time 5 minutes // Cook Time 12 minutes*

*Servings 2 // Temp 200°C or 390°F // No Skill Requires*

## Ingredients

Two burger patties or 10 oz. of beef

2 burger buns

2 slices of semi-hard cheese according to your desire

¼ teaspoon of burger seasoning

4 slice of tomato

2 leaves of lettuce

One pickle cucumber, sliced (optional)

2 teaspoons of ketchup

Pinch of salt

Pinch of pepper

## Directions

Put beef patties on a plate and add seasoning, salt, and pepper on top. If you are using mince, mix seasoning, salt, and pepper with mince and then make patties with hands.

Put in the Air Fryer and fry for 12 minutes at 200°C or 390°F and then check the burgers. If you want more fried meat, then cook burgers for further 5 minutes at 200°C or 390°F.

While meat is being cooked, prepare the buns. Spread 1 teaspoon of ketchup on the bottom of the buns.

Then using tongs put the hot fried meat on the bottom of the bun, place some slices of pickle cucumber on the patties, then a lettuce and 2 slice of tomato. Cover it with a bun.

Done.

## Simple Cheese Burger

*Prep Time 5 minutes // Cook Time 12 minutes*

*Servings 2 // Temp 200°C or 390°F // No Skill Requires*

### Ingredients

Two <u>burger patties</u> or 10 oz. of beef

2 burger buns

2 slices of semi-hard cheese according to your desire

¼ teaspoon of burger seasoning

2 teaspoons of ketchup

1 teaspoon of mustard

Salt and Pepper

## Directions

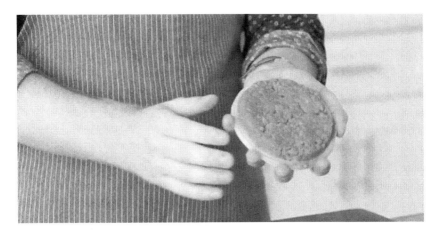

Put beef patties on a plate and add seasoning, salt, and pepper on top. If you are using mince, mix seasoning, salt, and pepper with mince and then make patties with hands.

Put in the Air Fryer and fry for 12 minutes at 200°C or 390°F and then check the burgers. If you want more fried meat, then cook burgers for further 5 minutes at 200°C or 390°F.

While meat is being cooked, prepare the buns. Spread 1 teaspoon of ketchup on the bottom of the bun. Spread 1/2 teaspoon of mustard on the top of the bun. Do the same with the second bun.

Then using tongs put the hot fried meat on the bottom of the bun, place a cheese slice on the patties, and cover it with a mustard bun.

## Gourmet Bacon Cheese Burger

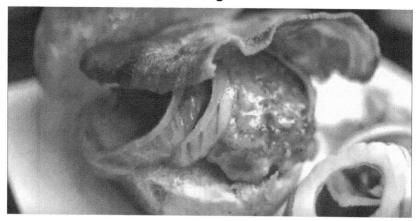

*Prep Time 5 minutes // Cook Time 5 minutes*

*Servings 1 // Temp 200° C or 390° F // No Skill Requires*

### Ingredients

Two <u>burger patties</u>

1 slices of bacons

Burger buns

2 slices of semi-hard cheese according to your desire

4 thin slices red onion

4 thin slices tomato

Salt and Pepper

Basil leaves

## Directions

Add patties and bacons into Air fryer

Fry for 5 minutes at 200°C or 390°F, then

Add cheese, onion and buns into Air fryer

Fry it for another 3 minutes at 200°C or 390°F

Then assemble burger put on beans patties, bacon, onion, tomato, cheese, basil and season with salt and pepper.

# Easy English Muffin Breakfast Sandwich (bacon, egg, cheese)

*Prep Time 5 minutes // Cook Time 5 minutes*

*Servings 1 // Temp 200° C or 390° F // No Skill Requires*

## Ingredients

1 English muffin

1 slice of bacon

1 slice of cheese

1 egg

1 pinch salt and pepper

Olive oil

## Directions

Put egg in oven proof cup and add oil spray before putting egg on there. Then add cup into Air fryer

Add muffin with cheese on top

Add bacon

Adjust for 6 minutes at 200 °C or 390 °F

Now assemble and plate them.

# CHAPTER _ DESSERT RECIPES

## Banana Sugar Cookies

*Prep Time 10 minutes // Cook Time 7+ minutes, it depending on the size of the basket*

*Servings20//Temp180°C or 360°F//Requires Minimum Skill*

**Ingredients**

2 cups of all-purpose flour

1 teaspoon of baking soda

1 teaspoon of ground cinnamon

¼ teaspoon of ground nutmeg

¼ teaspoon of salt

½ cup of vegan butter

¼ cup of shortening for baking

1 ¼ cup of light brown sugar

¼ cup of mashed banana

1 teaspoon of vanilla extract

¼ cup of granulated sugar (for rolling)

## Directions

### In a mixing bowl

Add the flour, baking soda, cinnamon, nutmeg, salt and mix it. Keep aside.

### In another mixing bowl

Add the butter and cream it until smooth. Use hand mixer.

Add brown sugar and whip until light and fluffy.

Add the mashed banana and vanilla and whip until accurately mixed.

Add the contents of the first mixing bowl.

Add the contents of the first mixing bowl and beat all ingredients in flour mixture.

Draw a tablespoon of dough, roll into a ball, and then roll in granulated sugar. Repeat with remaining dough.

Preheat Air fryer for 3 minutes at 180°C or 360°F

Place inside Air fryer basket a baking sheet and put cookies on sheet. Add dough balls 2" apart on cookie sheets.

Fry for 7 minutes at 180°C or 360°F

After 7 minutes put the cookies on a plate or cooling rack.

And then put the rest of the dough into Air fryer basket and repeat.

Remove cookies, cool and serve.

*Tip Do not over-bake; cookies will look puffy and soft (they let down as they cool). Allow cooling for 3 minutes on sheet before transferring to a cooling rack.*

*For this cookie, you need a well-mashed banana. Mash banana until texture of baby food using a fork. No lumps needed. You'll need only about half of a medium-sized banana to get 1/4 cup of mashed.*

# Butterless Strawberry Sugar Cookies

*Prep Time 10 minutes // Cook Time 12+12 minutes*

*Servings12//Temp180°C or 360°F//Requires Minimum Skill*

## Ingredients

3 cup of self-raising flour

1 cup of diced strawberries

1 cup of brown sugar

1 cup of caster sugar

6 fl.oz. of olive oil

2 fl.oz. of coconut oil

4 tablespoon of gluten free oats

1 tablespoon of honey

1 tablespoon of vanilla essence

2 medium eggs

## Directions

Clean the strawberries.

### In a mixing bowl

Add sugars (brown & caster) and the oils (coconut & olive) and whip until smooth and creamy with a hand mixer,

Add the vanilla essence, eggs and honey (optional),

Whip with the hand mixer again so that the eggs are well beaten into the cookie pastry.

Add little-by-little the flour and the oats and mix using a fork. Mix it until the cookie dough is well combined.

Add the strawberries and mix them into the dough with hands.


Preheat Air fryer for 3 minutes at 180°C or 360°F

Place inside Air fryer basket a baking sheet and put cookies on sheet.

Fry for 12 minutes at 180°C or 360°F

After 12 minutes put the cookies on a plate or cooling rack.

And then put the rest of the dough into Air fryer basket until you have 12 strawberry sugar cookies.

Remove, cool and serve.

## Chocolate Chips Cookies

*Prep Time 10 minutes // Cook Time 15 minutes*

*Servings12//Temp180°C or 360°F//Requires Minimum Skill*

## Ingredients

9 oz. of self-raising flour

5.5 oz. of butter

3 oz. of brown sugar

1.5 oz. of coconut sugar

4 tablespoon of honey (optional)

3 tablespoon of whole milk

1 tablespoon of cocoa powder

1 teaspoon of vanilla essence

3 oz. of chocolate chips

**Directions**

*In a mixing bowl*

Add butter, brown sugar and coconut sugar.

Blend it using a hand mixer. Butter and sugar must be well mixed and should be light and fluffy.

Add the flour, milk, cocoa powder, vanilla essence, honey (optional) and mix well with a fork.

Add chop chips or crushed chocolate in the cookie mix.


Sprinkle flour on hands so that the cookie mixture won't stick

Mix well with hands for a minute and making sure everything is well mixed.

Roll out into 12 small cookies.


Preheat Air fryer for 3 minutes at 180°C or 360°F

Place inside Air fryer basket a baking sheet and put cookies on sheet.

Fry for 15 minutes at 180°C or 360°F

Remove, cool and serve.


*Note Depending on the size of your Air fryer basket, you may have to repeat the frying procedure several times*

# Fruit Cake

*Prep Time 20 minutes // Cook Time 15 minutes*

*Servings 4 // Temp 180° C or 360° F // Requires Specific Skill*

## Ingredients

3 ½ oz. of all-purpose flour

3 ½ oz. of sugar powder

3 ½ oz. of butter

2 small eggs

½ teaspoon of vanilla essence

3 ½ oz. of candied fruit

¼ teaspoon of caraway seeds

Pinch of ginger powder

Pinch of cinnamon powder

Pinch of baking powder

## Directions

Slightly oil a round cake form and line it with a double layer of baking parchment.

### *In a mixing bowl*

Add butter and whip the butter with a hand mixer.

Once the butter gets soft, add little by little powdered sugar and mix it until light and fluffy.

Add little vanilla essence and egg mixture and whip it.

### *In another bowl*

Add flour, candied fruit, caraway seeds, ginger powder, cinnamon powder, baking powder and mix well.

Add the flour mixture into the butter mixture and slowly mix well at cut and fold mixing method with spatula.

Place the resulting mixture in round cake form

Preheat the Air fryer for 3 minutes at 180° C or 360° F.

Pull the round cake form in Air fryer basket and fry for 15 minutes at 180° C or 360° F

After 15 minutes, remove the cake form, insert a skewer into the cake and if it comes out clean take cake out and cold. Fry for another 5 minutes, if the skewer comes out with sticky dough.

Sprinkle some powdered sugar on cake top before cutting.

# Gluten Free Coconut Lime Cupcakes

*Prep Time 15 minutes // Cook Time 20 minutes*
*Servings 6 // Temp 180 °C or 360 °F // Requires Specific Skill*

## Ingredients

½ cup of coconut flour

½ cup of coconut oil, melted

1/3 cup of pure maple syrup

1/3 cup of coconut milk (not canned)

3 large eggs,

1 tablespoon of fresh lime juice

1/3 cup of shredded coconut, unsweetened

½ teaspoon of sea salt

½ teaspoon of baking soda

### For The Icing

1 cup of heavy cream or coconut cream

1/3 cup of pure maple syrup

1 teaspoon of vanilla extract

Zest of 1 lime

## Directions

### *In a mixing bowl*

Add eggs, coconut oil, maple syrup, coconut milk and lime juice and mix using a hand blender.

### *In another bowl*

Add coconut flour, shredded coconut, salt and baking soda and mix well using spatula or spoon.

Add the contents of the first bowl to the second bowl and blend all ingredients well

Spoon cupcake batter into each cupcake liner about ¾ way up and put into Air fryer basket.

Fry the cupcakes for 10 minutes at 160°C or 320°F and then for a further 10 minutes at 180°C or 360°F.

When the cupcakes are done allow them to cool down for 10 minutes on a plate.

### *In a third bowl*

Add the cream, maple syrup, vanilla and lime zest and whip until cream forms soft peaks using a hand mixer.

Add the icing on cupcakes top with a spoon.

Let cool cupcakes with icing in refrigerator.

Decorate with a lime slice before serving.

# Milk Powder Nuggets Soaked in Rose Syrup

*Prep Time 20 minutes // Cook Time 5 minutes*

*Servings 8-12//Temp 140°C or 280°F//Requires Specific Skill*

## Ingredients

2 cup powdered milk (*please refer notes)

6-8 tablespoon of milk (few tbsp. more or less, the dough should be smooth)

1 tablespoon of canola oil (or ghee, for dough and spray)

4 oz. almond or pistachio (crushed, for garnish)

1 tablespoon of unsalted butter (or use ghee butter organic grass fed - Clarified Butter)

½ teaspoon of baking powder.

1 tablespoon of all-purpose flour

2 tablespoons of semolina (fine, soaked in milk for 10 minutes)

*For Rose Syrup*

½ teaspoon of rose water

1 ½ cup of sugar

2 cup of water

1 teaspoon of lime juice

- *Notes: Milk Powder: Different brands of milk powders and different consistency (whole fat or lite) needs a different amount of milk to make a smooth dough. For this recipe I used 2 cups of lite milk. When using full fat, I use about 1.5 cups. You can adjust milk powder or add more milk until dough comes together, should not be dry or too wet too sticky. If dough gets too wet, leave aside for some time until milk powder absorbs the liquid (milk).*
*1 cup milk powder lite = about 125 grams;*
*1 cup milk powder whole = about 140 grams*

## Directions

Soak semolina in a bowl with 3 tablespoons water (or milk) and put aside.

### *In a wide bowl*

Add 2 cup of powdered milk and ½ tsp. of baking powder, and then mix well.

Add 1 tbsp. of cold butter diced in chunks (or ghee if using) and 1 tbsp. canola oil (or ghee if using).

Rub with hands to spread fat in milk powder.

Add soaked semolina and 1 tbsp. all-purpose flour, and mix with hand to combine.

Add milk a little bit at a time until it makes smooth dough. Don't knead to make the dough. Just use gentle pressure to bring everything together. Cover with kitchen towel and set aside for 10 minutes to rest.

*Tip: The dough should not be very dry, and not wet. The dough should not easily tear in your hands. It should become sticky and break with a little effort of the hands.*

Divide rested dough about into 20 even pars and put it on a plate.

With clean hands roll each part to make a ball. Make certain it is smooth from all sides, no cracks seeable. If dough sticks to hand, wash hand, wipe dry and repeat rolling again.

Preheat the Air fryer for 3 minutes at 140 °C or 280 °F.

Put the balls in the Air fryer then spray the oil on top and fry them for 5 minutes at 140 °C or 280 °F. After that, remove balls onto a plate. If you want more golden brown, you can fry for 3 minutes more at the same temperature.

Drop the balls in the sugar syrup and soak it for 15 minutes.

Balls are ready when soaked most of the syrup and look heavier than their size and are wet and porous due to soaking sugar syrup.

Garnish with almond flakes and serve it.

## Rose Syrup

You can make the rose syrup by yourself or <u>buy it</u>

If you make syrup yourself, then in a saucepan mix sugar and water, add lime juice. Heats until sugar have dissolved and boil for 3 minutes. Then mix in rose water and set aside.

*Tip: Storage and Re-Heating Instructions: Balls will stay good in the refrigerator, in an air-tight container for up to 1 week. To reheat just air fry for 1 minute at 180°C or 360°F, or microwave with syrup for 30 seconds.*

*Lime/lemon juice in syrup helps to prevent caking of sugar syrup. Don't miss that!*

*If you ever end up making a too hard or dry balls batch. Never throw them away. Just microwave with syrup for 30 seconds and they will be as soft as they should be.*

# Nutty Almond Butter Cookies

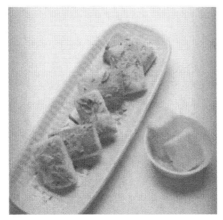

*Prep Time 20 minutes // Cook Time 7 minutes*

*Servings 12//Temp180°C or 355°F // Requires Specific Skill*

## Ingredients

4 oz. of butter

2 oz. of icing sugar

¼ teaspoon of almond essence

6 oz. all-purpose flour

2 tablespoon of nuts (almonds, cashew nuts, filbert)

## Directions

### In a mixing bowl

Add the butter and cream it well using spatula or hand mixer.

Add icing sugar, cream with butter until soft.

Add almond essence and mix.

Add flour and mix to make dough.

Using rolling pin, roll the dough and make a rectangle shape about 1 inch high.

Sprinkle some crushed nuts over the flat dough and roll once, so that the nuts pressed into the dough.

Cut dough into squares or desired shapes.

Preheat the Air fryer for 3 minutes at 180°C or 360°F

Put the cookies in the basket and fry for 7-8 minutes at 180°C or 360°F

Then remove cookies, cool and serve.

# Portuguese Egg Tart

*Prep Time 30 minutes // Cook Time 9 minutes*

*Servings 2 // Temp 200° C or 390° F // Requires Specific Skill*

## Ingredients

1 cup of granulated sugar

1 tablespoons of all-purpose flour

¾ cup whole milk (separate out ¼ cup)

1 cinnamon stick

1/3 cup of water

¼ teaspoon of vanilla extract

3 egg yolks

1 previously bought or made <u>puff pastry</u> sheet (11 oz. /310 grams)

**Directions**

### *In a mixing bowl:*

Add ¼ cup of milk

Add ¼ teaspoon of vanilla extract

Add 1 tablespoon of flour

Whisk into a smooth texture

### *In a sauce pan:*

Warm ½ cup of milk and add to the big bowl

### *In a big bowl:*

Whisk in the warm milk

### *In another sauce pan:*

Add 1/3 cup of water,

Add ½ cup of sugar,

Add 1 cinnamon stick and bring it to boil.

Discard cinnamon stick.


Separate 3 egg yolks.

### *Back to the big bowl:*

Pour and whisk sugar syrup into the big bowl

Pour and whisk in egg yolks,

Whisk it into a smooth texture and then pour custard into a jug with a spout.

### Mold the puff pastry

Roll out the puff pastry sheet and cut them into ½ inch length.

Butter custard tins

Flatten the pastry piece by using thumbs and index fingers,

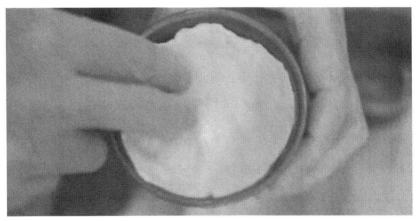

Mold flattens pastry puff pieces onto the cupcake tin cups.

Pour custard into tins – ¾ full.

Fry the Natas for 9 minutes in 200° C or 390° F or until brown tops appear.

## Soft Chocolate Cookies

*Prep Time 5 minutes // Cook Time 8 minutes*

*Servings 12//Temp 180°C or 360°F//Requires Minimum Skill*

## Ingredients

6 oz. of self-raising flour

3.5 oz. of butter

2.5 oz. of brown sugar

3.5 oz. of chocolate

2 tablespoon of honey

1 tablespoon of milk

## Directions

Crack up your chocolate on cutting board so that they are a mix of medium and tiny chocolate chunks. Use for this a rolling pin. Chocolate should be frozen to crack well. Keep aside.

*In a large bowl* (step-by-step)

Add butter and whip it until soft using hand mixer,

Add the sugar and cream with whipped butter until they are light and furry,

Add and stir the honey,

Add flour and mix well.

Add the chocolate.

And the milk and stir well.

Preheat Air fryer for 3 minutes at 180°C or 360°F

Place inside Air fryer basket a baking sheet and put cookies on sheet.

Fry for 6 minutes at 180°C or 360°F,

Then reduce at 160°C or 320°F and fry for 2 minutes.

Remove, cool and serve.

## Vanilla Muffins

*Prep Time 20 minutes // Cook Time 10 minutes*

*Servings 3//Temp 180°C or 360°F// Requires Specific Skill*

## Ingredients

4 oz. of butter

4 oz. of sugar powdered or Icing sugar

4 oz. of flour

¼ teaspoon of Vanilla Essence

2 not large eggs

Pinch of baking powder

2 oz. of oats

1 tablespoon of raisins

## Directions

### *In a mixing bowl,*

Add the butter, sugar and blend well with hand blender until soft.

Add vanilla essence and beaten eggs little by little and blend until mixed well.

### *In another small bowl,*

Add in the flour, baking powder, oats, raisins and mix well.

Add the flour mixture to the butter mixture and mix at cut and fold mixing method with spatula.

Line the muffin molds with paper or foil liners or you can use silicone muffin cups

Fill each mold with some batter and keep aside.

Preheat the Air fryer for 3 minutes at 180° C or 360° F

Pull the muffin molds in Air fryer basket and fry for 10 minutes at 180° C or 360° F

Remove, cool and serve

# CHAPTER _ SIDE DISHES AND SNACK RECIPES

## Crispy Homemade Nachos

*Prep Time 20 minutes // Cook Time 7 minutes*

*Servings 2 //Temp 180°C or 360°F // Requires Specific Skill*

**Ingredients**

½ cup of sweet corn

1 cup of all-purpose flour

Salt at taste

½ teaspoon of chilli powder

1 tablespoon of butter

½ cup of water

## Directions

### *In blender,*

Add little water to the fresh sweet corn and grind to a paste.

### *In a mixing bowl,*

Add all-purpose flour, salt, chilli powder, butter and mix the ingredients well.

Add the sweet corn mass and mix well.

Knead well to make stiff dough.

### *On a table or Pastry Mat,*

With help of rolling pin, fug some flour on the table and roll the dough into a thin sheet. Cut them into desired shapes with pizza cutter.

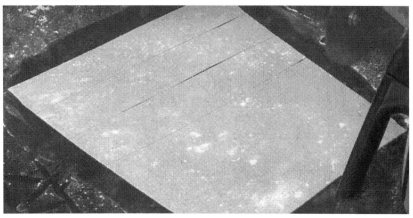

Put one piece of dough on top of the other and cut into triangles

Preheat the Air fryer for 3 minutes at 180°C or 360°F

Spray oil on a basket and drop the nachos in the Air fryer

Fry for 6 - 7 minutes at 180°C or 360°F

*Tips Serve with fresh homemade salsa.*

# Cheese and Spinach Stuffed Snacks

*Prep Time 20 minutes // Cook Time 7 minutes*
*Servings 2 // Temp 180° C or 360° F // Requires Specific Skill*

## Ingredients
### For the stuffing
½ cup of sweet corn
2 oz. of spinach, boiled and chopped
2 oz. of Mozzarella cheese, grated
1 oz. of any semi-soft cheese at your taste, grated
½ teaspoon of garlic, finely chopped
½ of medium onion, chopped
Salt to taste (not many, because the salt there is in the cheese)
1 tablespoon of breadcrumb
¼ teaspoon of black pepper, freshly crushed
Pinch of nutmeg powder (optional)

### For the outer casing
1 cup of all-purpose flour
Pinch of baking powder
1 teaspoon of chilli flakes

¼ teaspoon of basil or oregano

Salt - to taste

1 glass of buttermilk

## Directions

### *For making stuffing*

### *In a mixing bowl*

Add in all the ingredients for stuffing, mix well and keep aside.

### *For making the outer casing*

### *In another mixing bowl*

Add the flour, baking powder, pinch of salt, chilli flakes, basil or oregano and mix using a hand.

Add little by little buttermilk and knead into soft dough.

Take a rest the dough for a while (about 30 minutes) Dust some flour on the table, take some dough and roll into a thin sheet.

Cut the edges and cut dough sheet into squares about 4" on 4"

Fill in the stuffing on one side of the square.

Brush little water on the edges of the square,

Fold and seal the pillows by fingers.

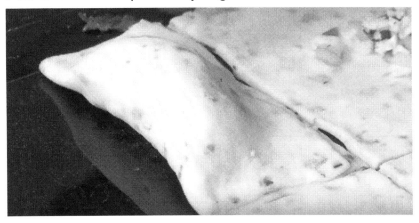

### In a medium bowl

Make a liquid mixture of water and flour and keep aside.

### In a plate put breadcrumbs,

Dip the pillow into flour mixture, remove and coat with bread crumbs and keep aside.

Preheat Air fryer for 3 minutes at 180°C or 360°F

Put your snacks in Air fryer and fry them for 4 minutes at 180°C or 360°F

After four minutes, open the tray and brush or spray snacks with little oil on both sides and fry for another 2-3 minutes at 180°C or 360°F

# French Fries

*Prep Time 5 minutes // Cook Time 15 minutes*

*Servings 2 // Temp 205°C or 400°F// No Skill Requires*

## Ingredients

3 medium russet potatoes

1 ½ tablespoons of coconut oil

½ teaspoon Onion Powder

½ teaspoon Garlic Power

¼ teaspoon of salt

¼ teaspoon of pepper

## Directions

Peel and slice potatoes into strips about 0.5 inches wide and 4 inches long.

Soak potatoes in a bowl of fresh water for 30 minutes.

Drain water and dry potatoes using paper towels.

Spray on potatoes coconut oil then sprinkle seasonings that would coat well.

Put potatoes strips into Air Fryer basket and fry for 10 minutes at 205°C or 400°F. After 10 minutes remove the basket and stir the potatoes. Be careful, HOT, use a tongs or spatula.

Fry for another 10 minutes at 205°C or 400°F and then remove the basket and stir the potatoes again.

If you want more crispy potatoes then fry for another 10 minutes at 205°C or 400°F

# Full English Fry-up Breakfast

*Prep Time: 5 minutes // Cook Time: 15 minutes*

*Servings 1 // Temp 180°C or 355°F// No Skill Requires*

## Ingredients

2 - 3 sausages

2 – 3 rashers

1 large egg

2 pieces of black pudding

1/3 cup of milk

1 oz. of butter

Salt and pepper

## Directions

Add in oven proof cup one egg, 1/3 cup of milk, 1 oz. of butter, pinch salt and pepper and mix well with a fork.

Preheat Air fryer for 2 minutes at 180°C or 355°F.

Place sausages and black pudding in Air fryer basket, insert Rack for Air fryer and add rashers on rack.

Put basket into Air fryer and fry for 10 minutes, after that get the basket and remove rashes.

Add oven proof cup with egg mixed with butter and milk on rack and put basket back in Air fryer or final 5 minutes.

Remove after 2 minutes and stir the egg, put basket back for last 3 minutes.

# Parmesan Dill Pickle Chips with Ranch Dressing

*Prep Time 15 minutes // Cook Time 20 minutes*

*Servings 4//Temp 205°C or 400°F//No Skill Requires*

## Ingredients

2 lb. whole large dill pickles (32 oz. jar)

2 medium eggs

6 oz. of panko breadcrumbs

3 oz. of grated Parmesan

¼ teaspoon of dried dill weed

### For Ranch Dressing

1/2 cup mayonnaise and 1/2 cup sour cream (or 1 cup sour cream)

1/2 cup milk

1 teaspoon of dill weeds; dried or fresh, fine chopped

1/4 teaspoon of Himalayan salt

1/4 teaspoon of black pepper, fresh ground

1/2 teaspoon of garlic powder

1/2 teaspoon of onion powder

2 teaspoons of raw apple cider vinegar

1/8 teaspoon of cayenne pepper

## Directions

## Make a Ranch Dressing

### *In a mixing bowl*

Add all ingredients and blend well with whisk.

You can store in for refrigerator for up to five days.

## Make a pickle chips

Slice the large pickles diagonally into middle slices, about 1/4 inches.

Place on paper towels and wipe out to dry.

*In a plate,* beat the eggs until smooth.

*In a mixing bowl*

Add the breadcrumbs, dried Parmesan, and dill weed, and then mix it well.

Dip the pickle slices into the beaten egg, remove any over egg and then drop into the Panko mixture.

Spray oil on coated pickles and add half of them into the Air Fryer basket and fry for 10 minutes at 205°C or 400°F

Then put the rest of the pickles into Air fryer and fry the same way.

Serve immediately and dip pickle chips into Ranch dressing.

*If you have an XL Air fryer, you may fry all the pickles in one part.*

# Papad Cheese in Paneer. Simple vegetarian snack

*Prep Time 15 minutes // Cook Time 5 minutes*

*Servings 1// Temp 180°C or 360°F // Requires Specific Skill*

## Ingredients

1 cup crumbled Paneer (cottage cheese)

Salt to taste

1 tablespoon grated garlic

1 teaspoon chilli powder

2 teaspoon tomato ketchup

1/4 cup all-purpose flour

3/4 cup crushed papad

Olive oil for spray

## Directions

Put the paneer in a plate and knead well. *(Also, you can buy a paneer in a briquette form, which will need to be cut.)*

Add the salt, garlic, chilli powder, tomato ketchup and mix well.

Divide the mixture into 9 equal portions and roll each portion into a 50 mm. (2") long cylindrical shape. Keep aside.

Add the ¼ cup of all-purpose flour in a bowl, then add ½ cup water and mix well.

Dip each roll into the flour-water paste and then roll in the crushed paneer.

Preheat Air Fryer for 4 minutes at 180°C or 360°F

Spray oil on paneer and put it in Air fryer.

Fry them for 5 minutes at 180°C or 360°F

.

*Tip: Paneer is a traditional, full-fat, soft cheese used in Indian cooking. Paneer is a quick-ripening cheese which is coagulated by the action of an acid in milk and not by using rennet. This vegetarian cheese is pressed until the texture is firm, similar to tofu. An excellent source of protein, paneer makes an excellent meat substitute.*

**Real Chips**

*Prep Time 10 minutes // Cook Time: 25 minutes*

*Servings 4 // Temp: 200° C or 390° F // No Skill Requires*

**Ingredients**

2 lbs. of potatoes

1 teaspoon of salt

1 teaspoon of pepper

1 tablespoon of <u>extra-virgin olive oil</u>

1 teaspoon of garlic powder

1 tablespoon of paprika

## Directions

Peel and wash potatoes, then cut potatoes roughly into your desired shape,

Place the chopped potatoes in bowl of water,

Remove potatoes from water and dry off with a paper towels,

Put back potatoes into empty bowl,

Sprinkle with salt, pepper, garlic powder and paprika,

Add extra virgin olive oil and mix well.

Place in Air fryer basket,

Fry for 25 minutes at 200° C or 390° F

## Onion Rings with Sauce

*Prep Time 10 minutes // Cook Time: 10 minutes*

*Servings 2 // Temp 190°C or 375°F // No Skill Requires*

### Ingredients

2 - 3 big onions or 1 lbs. Frozen Onion Rings

1 cup of <u>All Purpose Flour</u>

1 tablespoon of <u>Paprika</u>

1 tablespoon of <u>Baking Powder</u>

1 cup of milk

1 large egg

5 oz of <u>Breadcrumbs</u>

Salt and pepper

## Directions

Cut the onion and divide it into rings. Onion rings should be about 0,5 inches thick.

## In first bowl:

Add 1 cup of All Purpose Flour,

Add 1 tablespoon of Paprika,

Add 1 teaspoon of salt,

Add 1 tablespoon of Baking Powder

Mix well with a spoon, and envelope the onion rings in the resulting mixture of spices.

## In second bowl

Add 1 cup of milk

Add 1 egg

Pint salt and pepper

Mix well with a whisk,

Strew the spices mix of the first bowl

Mix well with a whisk to a homogeneous mass.

Envelope the onion rings in the resulting mass.

**In first bowl (already empty):**

Add 5 oz of Breadcrumbs

Envelope the onion rings in the Breadcrumbs.


Add onion rings to basket and put in Air fryer

Fry for 10 minutes at 190° C or 375° F

Plate it and enjoy.


**Make the sauce**

Whisk up the next ingredients in a bowl,

1/2 cup of Mayonnaise,

2 tablespoons of Heinz Ketchup,

1 tablespoon of Horseradish Root,

½ teaspoon of paprika.


*Tip: For a little more spice in the sauce, add a touch of paprika, oregano, pepper, cayenne.*

# Ham and Cheese Toaster

*Prep Time 1 minute // Cook Time: 15 minutes*

*Servings 1 // Temp 180° C or 360° F // No Skill Requires*

## Ingredients

2 slice of bread

1 oz. of butter

Slice of ham

2 oz. grated cheese

## Directions

Butter both sides of bread

Add ham to inside,

Add cheese to outside.

Place sandwich into basket and fry for 15 minutes at 180° C or 360° F

# Chicken Rice Balls

*Prep Time 20 minutes // Cook Time 8 minutes*

*Servings 3 // Temp 180°C or 360°F // Requires Specific Skill*

## Ingredients

2 cup of cooked rice

8 oz. of chicken curry (roasted chicken fillet with curry spice) or kebabs fries etc., chopped

1 teaspoon of mint leaves, chopped

1 tablespoon of coriander leaves, chopped

1 teaspoon of chicken spice mix powder or any spice for chicken

2 egg yolks

1 cup of breadcrumbs (for coating)

2 beaten eggs

1 cup of all-purpose flour

**Directions**

*In a mixing bowl,*

Add two cups of rice and any left-over chicken curry or kebabs fries etc,

Add finely chopped mint and coriander leaves, spice for chicken, egg yolks and mix all ingredients well with spatula.

Dust some flour in your hands and shape this mixture into balls about 2 - 3" around, and keep aside.

Put three soup plates on the table, first plate with beaten egg, second with flour and third with breadcrumbs.

Take a chicken ball and roll over in the beaten egg and then in the flour, repeat once again in the beaten egg and finally coat with breadcrumbs.

Complete the same operation with all the chicken balls and keep aside.

Preheat the Air fryer for 3 minutes at 180°C or 360°F

Fry for 8 minutes at 180°C or 360°F

Serve with favorite sauce.

# CHAPTER _ VEGETABLE RECIPES

## Banana Peppers Stuffed

*Prep Time 20 minutes // Cook Time 10 minutes*

*Servings 2 // Temp 180°C or 360°F // Requires Specific Skill*

## Ingredients

4 pcs of large banana peppers

1 cup of cottage cheese

1 cup of mozzarella cheese

½ teaspoon of garlic finely chopped

1 teaspoon of red bell pepper finely chopped

1 teaspoon of yellow bell pepper finely chopped

1 tablespoon of spinach boiled and chopped

1 pinch of nutmeg powder

¼ teaspoons of pepper powder

¼ cup of all-purpose flour

1 cup of breadcrumbs

2 tablespoons of oil (as required)

## Directions

Wash and deseed the banana peppers.

### *In a bowl*

Add cottage cheese, mozzarella cheese, finely chopped garlic, red and yellow bell pepper, boiled and chopped spinach, a pinch of nutmeg powder, crushed pepper and mix it well.

Farce the prepared mess into banana peppers.

### *In another bowl*

Add all-purpose flour and add water to make a liquid batter.

Take the farce banana pepper and dip it into the liquid batter and coat with breadcrumbs and place it aside.

Two minutes beyond coat banana pepper with breadcrumbs again.

Preheat the Air fryer for 4 minutes at 180° C or 360° F

Put in Air fryer the stuffed banana peppers and fry them for 5 minutes at 180°C or 360°F.

After five minutes pull out the basket and spray oil, then refry the banana peppers for 4 minutes at 180°C or 360°F.

# Crispy Baby Corn in Sesame

*Prep Time 10 minutes // Cook Time 6 minutes*

*Servings 2//Temp 180°C or 360°F //Requires Minimum Skill*

## Ingredients

8 pcs of baby corns

1 teaspoon of red chili paste

¼ teaspoon of soya sauce

½ teaspoon of green chili paste

½ teaspoon of ginger, finely chopped

½ teaspoon of garlic, finely chopped

¼ teaspoon of green chilies

1 bunch of coriander leaves (optional)

1 pinch of star anise powder (optional)

1 pinch of salt

1 tablespoon of tomato ketchup

1 tablespoon of cornstarch

2 tablespoons of sesame seeds

## Directions

Soak 8 wooden skewers in water for about 10 -20 minutes and then remove. It is necessary that wood does not start to smolder in Air Fryer.

Insert wooden skewers into each baby corn. Pierce baby corns along the entire length and keep aside.

*Tip Match the size of the skewers and your Air fryer basket. If necessary, the sticks can be shortened.*

### *In a mixing bowl,*

Add red chili paste, soya sauce, star anise powder (optional), green chili paste, ginger, garlic, green chilies, coriander leaves (optional), salt, tomato ketchup, cornstarch

Mix all ingredients well together to make a fine sauce.

Take the baby corn stick and coat it well with the sauce mix and then roll it in the sesame seeds.

Repeat the same with all the baby corn sticks and keep aside.

Preheat the Air Fryer for 4 minutes at 180°C or 360°F

Put the baby corn sticks into Air fryer and fry for 6 minutes at 180°C or 360°F

Serve hot with favorite sauce.

# Cut Okra Fried

*Prep Time 5 minutes // Cook Time 5 minutes*

*Servings 2 // Temp 205° C or 400° F // No Skill Requires*

## Ingredients

1 lb. of cut okra (frozen or fresh)

1 large egg

3 tablespoon of bread crumbs

½ teaspoon of garlic salt

½ teaspoon of salt

½ teaspoon of pepper

## Directions

Whisk the egg with ½ teaspoon of salt and ½ teaspoon of pepper.

Put the cut okra into the bowl, add the whisked egg and mix well.

In the separate bowl mix 3 tablespoons of bread crumbs and ½ teaspoon of garlic salt.

Add the egg okra to the breadcrumbs and wrap.

Spray oil on okra and place it in Air fryer.

Fry for 5 minutes at 205° C or 400° F

Enjoy with homemade mayonnaise or your favorite sauce.

# Hasselback Cheese Potatoes

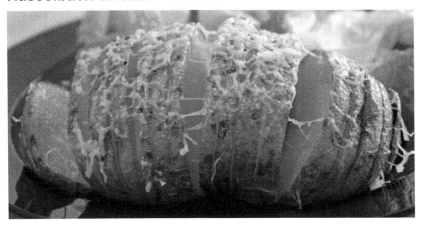

*Prep Time 5 minutes // Cook Time 25 minutes*

*Servings 4 // Temp 180° C or 360° F // Requires Specific Skill*

## Ingredients

4 large potatoes

2 oz. of cheddar or any hard/semi-hard cheese

1 tablespoon of olive oil

1 tablespoon of garlic puree

1 tablespoon of fresh rosemary

1 tablespoon of parsley

Pinch of Salt & Pepper

## Directions

Place four large potatoes on a chopping board. Slice all vegetables using the Hasselback potatoes method.

Strew salt, pepper, and parsley onto the potatoes (so that some of it makes its way into the gaps).
Place in the Air fryer basket the grill pan and put the potatoes and fry for about 15 minutes at 180° C or 360° F.

The potatoes will be HOT!
After 15 minutes take from the Air Fryer with an oven glove or tongs and put them back on the chopping board.

### *In a mixing bowl*
Add garlic, olive oil, and the fresh rosemary.
Spread the mixture down the bottom, top, and sides of the potatoes with fingers, so it will go down the slits.
Then, strew cheese on top.

Put into the basket and fry again for 10 minutes at 180° C or 360° F.

# Spanish Spicy Potatoes

*Prep Time 10 minutes // Cook Time 25 minutes*
*Servings 4 // Temp 180°C or 360°F // Requires Specific Skill*

## Ingredients
3 large potatoes peeled and sliced into wedges
1 small onion peeled and diced
3.5 oz. of tomato sauce
1 tomato thinly diced
1 tablespoon of red wine vinegar
2 tablespoon of olive oil
1 teaspoon of paprika
1 teaspoon of chili powder
2 teaspoon of coriander
2 teaspoon of thyme
½ teaspoon of basil
1 teaspoon of oregano
1 teaspoon of rosemary
1/8 teaspoon of salt
¼ teaspoon of pepper

## Directions

Slice potatoes and spray the oil on potatoes wedges.
Put them in the basket and fry for about 15 minutes at 180°
C or 360° F

### *Make sauce in a mixing bowl*

Add rest of the ingredients and mix well with spoon or using
spatula.

Pull out the potatoes when fry.
Using a baking dish put the tomato sauce in Air fryer for 8
minutes at 180° C or 360° F.

When it fry, pour the sauce onto the potatoes and serve.

# Spinach Soya Nuggets

*Prep Time 10 minutes // Cook Time 7 minutes*

*Servings 3 // Temp 180° C or 360° F // Requires Specific Skill*

## Ingredients

1 cup of soya granules, soaked in water

½ cup of spinach, grated

1 cup of potato, boiled & grated

½ teaspoon of green chilies, finely chopped

½ of small onion, finely chopped

1 tablespoon of coriander leaves, finely chopped

½ tablespoon of mint leaves, finely chopped

¼ teaspoon of turmeric powder

½ teaspoon of chili powder

¼ teaspoon of coriander powder

¼ teaspoon of cumin powder

1 tablespoon of all-purpose flour

2 tablespoons of bread crumbs

Salt to taste
Water as required

## Directions
### *In a mixing bowl*
Add soya granules (soaked in water for a while and then drain off the water),
Add spinach, boiled and grated
Add potato boiled and grated,
Add green chilies, onion, coriander leaves, mint leaves, turmeric, chili powder, coriander powder, cumin powder, and salt to taste.
Add little breadcrumb if you feel the mixture is too moist.
Mix all the ingredients well and shape them into nugget form.

### *In a small bowl*
Make a batter with all-purpose flour and water.

Dip the nuggets in the batter and then roll over the bread crumbs coating them well and keep aside.

Preheat the Air fryer for 3 minutes at 180°C or 360°F

Put the nuggets in the basket and fry for about 3-4 minutes at 180°C or 360°F

Then remove and spray them with little oil and fry it again for 2-3 minutes at 180°C or 360°F

# Sweet Cauliflower Pieces

*Prep Time 15 minutes // Cook Time 20 minutes*

*Servings4//Temp 180°C or 360°F//Requires Minimum Skill*

## Ingredients

1 cauliflower, about 2 lb.

1/3 cup of gluten-free oats

1/3 cup of all-purpose flour

1/3 cup of desiccated coconut (optional)

1 large egg, beaten

1 1/2 tablespoons of maple syrup

1 teaspoons of brown sugar

1 teaspoon of garlic puree

2 tablespoon of soy sauce

1/2 teaspoon of thyme powder

1/2 teaspoon of coriander powder

1/2 teaspoon of mustard powder

1/4 teaspoon of salt

1/4 teaspoon of pepper

**Directions**

Cut cauliflower into small pieces.

*In a mixing bowl*

Add oats, flour and coconut, salt and pepper and mix well.

*In a plate*, beat the eggs until smooth.

Season your cauliflower with coriander, thyme, salt, and pepper.

Dip the cauliflower pieces into the beaten egg, remove any over egg and then drop into the oats mixture.

Preheat Air Fryer for 3 minutes at 180° C or 360° F

Put the cauliflower in the basket and fry for 15 minutes at 180° C or 360° F

*While it is frying make the glazing syrup*

*In a mixing bowl*

Add maple syrup, brown sugar, garlic puree, soy sauce, mustard powder and mix well.

When the Air Fryer is done take the cauliflower out and put it all in the mixing bowl with your glazing syrup.

The cauliflower will be HOT! So, use the tongs and mix fried cauliflower pieces and glazing so that all is well coated.

Put back in the Air Fryer the cauliflower and fry for a further 5 minutes at 180° C or 360° F

Serve on a layer of lettuce.

*Tip: add a piece of parchment paper or baking mat into the Air fryer tray and the glazing mix will not drip down.*

## Thyme Fried Celeriac and Parsnips

*Prep Time 10 minutes // Cook Time 20 minutes*
*Servings 6 // Temp 200°C or 390°F // No Skill Requires*

### Ingredients

10 oz. parsnips

10 oz. celeriac

10 oz. 'butternut squash'

1 tablespoon of fresh thyme needles

1 tablespoon of olive oil

1/2 teaspoon of pepper

1/4 teaspoon of salt

## Directions

Peel the parsnips and celeriac. Cut the parsnips and celeriac into 1 inch cubes. Halve the 'butternut squash', remove the seeds and cut into cubes. (There's not necessary to peel it.)

## *In a mixing bowl*

Add cut vegetables, the thyme and olive oil, salt, and pepper and mix well.

Preheat the Air fryer for 5 minutes at 200°C or 390°F

Put the seasoned vegetables in the basket and fry for about 20 minutes at 200°C or 390°F

Stir the vegetables once while roasting.

## Wholesome Mediterranean Vegetables

*Prep Time 10 minutes // Cook Time 20 minutes*
*Servings 4 // Temp 180°C or 360°F // No Skill Requires*

### Ingredients

5 - 6 Cherry tomatoes

1 large zucchini, sliced to rings about ½ inch wide

2 medium Bell peppers cut to six wedges

1 large parsnip, diced

1 medium carrot, diced

1 medium red onion, cut to eight wedges

1/2 teaspoon of thyme

1 teaspoon of coriander

1 tablespoon of Brown sugar or tbsp. of maple syrup

1 teaspoon of Dijon mustard

2 teaspoons of garlic puree

3 oz. of olive oil

1/4 teaspoon of salt

1/4 teaspoon of pepper

## Directions

Peel and cut vegetables.

*In the Air Fryer basket* slice up the sliced zucchini and Bell pepper.

Then add diced parsnip and carrot, onion and add the cherry tomatoes whole while still on the vine for more flavors.

Sprinkle with oil and fry for 15 minutes at 180°C or 360°F

*In an oven-safe deep dish make the marinade*

Add the thyme, coriander, brown sugar or maple syrup, Dijon mustard, garlic puree, oil, salt and pepper and mix well.

The vegetables will be HOT! So, use the tongs when greens are fried and put them in the baking dish with the marinade.

Mix well so that all the vegetables are covered in the marinade.

Then put it again into Air fryer and fry for 5 minutes at 200°C or 390°F

## Zucchini Fryers

*Prep Time 5 minutes // Cook Time 15 minutes*

*Servings 2 // Temp 180°C or 360°F // No Skill Requires*

## Ingredients

2 Zucchinis (about 1 lb. at all)

2 Eggs

3 tablespoon of All Purpose Flour

3 tablespoon of Bread Crumbs

1/2 teaspoon of Garlic Salt

1 teaspoon of Dried Parsley

1 tablespoon of Shredded Parmesan

1 teaspoon of Paprika

## Directions

Cut the zucchini in thick slices about 3" in length and 1" in wide.

*In the first bowl:* Add all-purpose flour

**In a second bowl:** Beat eggs until stiff.

**In a third bowl:** Combine bread crumbs, garlic cloves, dried parsley, paprika and shredded parmesan. Stir until well combined.

Dip zucchinis in the flour then egg and lastly into the breadcrumbs mixture.

Spray oil on zucchini and place it in Air fryer.

Fry for 10 minutes at 200° C or 390° F

Enjoy with homemade mayonnaise or your favorite sauce.

I hope this book was convenient and useful for you
Thanks for reading.
Sincerely,
Mia Douglas

Made in the USA
Columbia, SC
04 February 2018